International Reorganization and
American Economic Policy

International Reorganization and American Economic Policy

Leonard A. Rapping
Professor of Economics, University of Massachusetts

NEW YORK UNIVERSITY PRESS
Washington Square, New York

First published 1988 in the USA by
NEW YORK UNIVERSITY PRESS
Washington Square
New York, NY 10003

© 1988 Leonard A. Rapping

Printed and bound in Great Britain by
A. Wheaton & Co. Ltd, Exeter

Library of Congress Cataloging-In-Publication Data

Rapping, Leonard A.
    International reorganization and American economic policy /
  Leonard A. Rapping.
       p. cm.
    Bibliography: p.
    Includes index.
    ISBN 0-8147-7407-5
    1. International Finance. 2. Economic history—1971– 3. United
States—Economic policy—1971–1981. 4. United States—Economic
policy—1981– 5. United States—Economic conditions—1971–1981.
6. United States—Economic conditions—1981– I. Title.
HG3881.R32 1988
338.973—dc19   88-28844
                                                                   CIP

To my parents, Joseph and Rose Rapping,
and all my other teachers

Contents

List of Tables

Preface*

These essays are about economic responses to new and rapidly transforming conditions of the global economy. The failure in Indochina, the emergence of parity in intercontinental missilry, the disintegration of the Bretton Woods system, the rise in the price of oil, the weakening of domestic political coalitions, the growth in the East Asian economies, the development of large budget and trade deficits in the United States, and the intensification of speculative fever – these are some of the more important developments which motivate action and necessitate a new global division of labour.

The required retrenchment and repositioning of American industry and the concomitant alterations in the distribution of both income and authority, have demanded that domestic and international economic institutions adapt and change. In the past fifteen years, then, American economic history is the story of rapid and sometimes painful social and economic change reflecting international repositioning and domestic restructuring.

Given the politics of opportunism and image, directing the restructuring of the economy by a rational, democratic regulatory process has proved impossible. As a result, the most significant economic, political and social event of this period has been the expanding domain of the unregulated market, the only feasible alternative given the breakdown in the decision-making capability of our political institutions. However, despite the current and unexpectedly long economic expansion in the United States, the outcome of the American restructuring effort remains problematic.

In these essays I employ the 'method of economics' which Keynes

*Written in December of 1987 in Waltham, Massachusetts.

referred to as an 'apparatus of mind' and a 'way of thinking'. The method has been developed over some 200 years and is nothing more or less than a problem-solving approach based on the presumption that a rational mode of inquiry can uncover certain empirical truths or statistical regularities even when the process under examination is subject to chance or, indeed, even when it is irrational. I was taught the method at UCLA and at the University of Chicago in the 1950s. My understanding of what I had learned was tested by my experiences at RAND in the early 1960s, enriched and expanded by my decade-long stay at Carnegie–Mellon, tempered by my encounters at the University of Massachusetts since the mid-1970s, and applied and modified by my experiences at diverse government and private agencies in Washington in the 1960s and again in the 1980s.

In this approach, the construction of economic models – whether thought of as abstract replicas of reality designed to capture the essence of a problem, or as econometric systems with stable structures and parameters to be identified and estimated for purposes of prediction – is not essential. Nor is it essential to assume optimizing agents. Admittedly, this assumption has considerable power. By pretending that the actions of organizations like corporations and governments can be assembled by analogy with rational individual behaviour, economists, political scientists and others are permitted to explain the actions of large institutions without detailed – indeed, without any – knowledge of these organizations. This is the Ricardian approach of classical economic reasoning. It is powerful because it permits action in the face of institutional ignorance. It is compromised when its practioners ignore institutional detail, or indeed, shun those who attempt to provide it.

Keep in mind that decision-making units in our economy are primarily large and small organizations and that these institutions are governed by behaviour not always decipherable in terms of the received theory of the firm or the household. As we have been repeatedly reminded in the writings Herbert Simon, the behaviour of these institutions must be carefully observed lest we fail to uncover systematic responses to specific events. When seen from the perspective of managerial science and behavioural theory, the economist's micro-foundations remind one of the old proverb: 'To make an assumption is to fool oneself.'

Behavioural theories, or what might more properly be called institutional theories, offer some promises in accounting for market behaviour, especially in tumultuous times. The research strategy underlying this approach is the 'case method', an approach that requires fieldwork and day-to-day experience. Of course, judgements must be made on the basis of limited information but this does not always require resorting to abstract reasoning. Wherever possible in these essays I have attempted to use whatever historical and institutional information was available to me.

It should also be stressed that the analysis in these essays assumes that the process of change cannot be understood in equilibrium terms, not even if the concept of dynamic equilibrium is employed. Instead, with constant, massive and unpredictable shocks, the system gropes from position to position. There is no correct position, for the concept of fundamentals is a chimera. This is not to deny the value of the equilibrium approach under certain circumstances, but only to suggest that it is not useful for the historical period under examination or for answering the questions posed in these essays.

In light of my previous research, particularly my competitive, equilibrium labour market studies with Robert Lucas, the above comments might seem somewhat inconsistent. I think not. Economics is the study of how social systems of production, distribution and consumption adapt to changing circumstances. As prices and wages change, as advertising campaigns are intensified, as technology evolves, institutions must adapt. Those which are flexible, profit and endure. Those which are not, wither and die.

Similarly, the important intellectual trait necessary for understanding a changing situation is the willingness to change one's mind, to alter the mental model, or its parameters, to accept the painful process of rethinking and relearning: in short, to be intellectually and emotionally adaptable. This is the key to survival for individuals as well as social systems. In the past fifteen years the situation has unfolded more rapidly than in the earlier, post-World War II years and I have adapted to these changes.

There is another issue raised in these essays tied not so much to matters of economic theory or method but rather to matters of political economy. Chicago and Milton Friedman had impressed on me an appreciation for the workings of an unregulated, market economy driven by self-interest and pecuniary rewards, and the belief that this form of social organization contributed significantly to prosperity, to stability, and to individual freedom—an especially important concern after the great victory against Hitler. I was deeply suspicious of the central planning systems in the Soviet Union and Eastern Europe. I was a libertarian who believed in unconstrained individual choice and in the power of rationality to improve a world populated by imperfect and imperfectible human beings.

There is much of this that I still accept. Markets are useful, pecuniary rewards are necessary, central planning is unadaptable, rationality is important, and people are imperfect. However, the combination of these ideas does not constitute an economic policy capable of guiding the American economy – let alone the world economy – towards a new global division of labour, one consistent with the new conditions that have developed in the past decade. It must be obvious to everyone that we have taken the unregulated market route not because regulation is unnecessary – witness the problem of maintaining confidence in our banking system – not because a market-based income distribution is motivationally optimal – witness the low personal savings rate and the poor productivity performance that continues in the service sector of the American economy – not because market prices always send the proper signals – witness the behaviour of exchange rates, interest rates and the price of common stocks – but rather because the events of the past fifteen years have greatly weakened public authority. The unregulated market emerged by default, not choice. In these essays it is argued that some regulation is necessary, especially in financial markets at home and abroad, and that we must construct the coalitions capable of building a consensus on this matter.

While at Massachusetts I have integrated into my own thinking some of my colleagues' ideas about political economy. I have developed a distinct preference for some market regulation, especially to protect both ecological and credit systems. I have developed a proper concern for those whose economic livelihoods will be threatened or destroyed in the process of American repositioning. I have developed intensified outrage at income inequities having little to do with incentives. I have developed a respect for the difficulty and importance of building a political coalition committed to democracy and justice when economic pressures mount. Despite these influences I remain unwilling to be bound by inflexible ideas that prevent me from thinking clearly and rationally about the complex economic process now in motion around the world.

Radical economists have developed theories that compete with the Keynesian and Lucasian theories of the business cycle. Their theoretical model of the business cycle is based on the empirical judgement that real wages outpace productivity when unemployment rates are low or that improved productivity requires the threat of unemployment. The model is grounded in class analysis. I find it misdirecting.

It is in periods of expanding, not contracting, employment when productivity expands most comfortably, suggesting that it is the 'sense of workmanship' combined with wage and status differentials, not the 'threat of the sack' that motivates workers.

Equally important, the theory does not contain a mechanism for inflation nor does it contain a credit-creation process. The monetary process can sustain an expansion long after profit conditions signal contraction, and the radical theory of the business cycle cannot therefore account for stagflation. It is monocausal and parochial in perspective. It ignores the role of important international matters such as oil pricing, trade penetration and financial integration.

While it shares these limitations with many other models, it suffers from its own unique limitation, it is built on a foundation of sand. An analysis based on class is irrelevent for a geographically, ethnically, religiously, linguistically, politically, emotionally and financially polyglot nation like the United States.

The more promising approach to inflation requires stress on the credit-creation process, the price and money wage-setting processes, and the larger forces that set these processes in motion. The convincing location for inflationary problems is not the domestic point of production, but the international sphere where procedures are necessary to order the global credit-creation process, the trade negotiation process, the oil price-setting process, and the peace process.

The correct and most fruitful view of the workplace and its relationship to the larger bureaucratic system of production is the behavioural theory of organizations laid out by Herbert Simon forty years ago, not an irrelevant class analysis or an analysis based on a rational, representative household and firm.

This of course raises the issue of the micro-foundations of macro-theory, a popular topic these days. Economists approach this problem by generalizing from the implied behaviour of a 'representative' and perfectly rational household or firm. The use of a representative individual is admittedly a powerful assumption, and it underlies much of our political and military analysis of the behaviour of nation-states. The idea is old. Some of the biblical stories of Abraham and Issac can be interpreted in terms of the corporate individual. None the less, this approach finesses the problem of how complex organizations overcome their internal political and informational barriers to rationality.

And, moreover, people are not perfectly rational nor are they always approximately rational. They make mistakes, they are creatures of habit or custom, they get angry, irrational and sometimes even silly. In short, they are not always predictable or rational. But they sometimes follow rules or traditions that help them to solve certain problems. A behavioural approach to decision-making involves the careful study of how organizations actually make decisions. This I think gives us a better opportunity to study macroeconomics from a micro-foundation.

The price level, the exchange rate, the price of common stocks and the interest rate are all macroeconomic variables that are best explained on the basis of behavioural rather than optimizing actions. There is, for example, widespread support for the view that the price level is simply a mark-up on variable costs. This is a proposition based on observing the behaviour of businessmen, not on introspection by the theoretician about appropriate behaviour in a pricing situation.

Since the mid-1970s, the gyrations in exchange rates and stock prices are determined more by speculative fever, which drifts from market to market, than by the forces implied by the theories of purchasing power parity, interest rate parity, or discounted expected profits. Nor can traditional optimizing theory based on rational behaviour account for either the high interest rates or the collapse of monetary velocity in the 1980s. Nor can standard rational maximizing behaviour explain the low personal savings rate in the United States in the 1980s, nor can it account for the continuing and large trade deficit in the same period.

The behavioural approach seems to offer some promise in accounting for market behaviour in the tumultuous years since the first oil price shock. The essays in this book draw freely from this theoretical perspective. My current approach is far removed from my earlier thinking on business cycles. It is worthwhile therefore to say something more about equilibrium business cycle theory, particularly that branch of theory based on rational expectations.

I had worked on this approach in the 1960s, a time when the intellectual challenge in economics was to account for an inverse relationship between inflation and unemployment. The disequilibrium Keynesian model has no implication on this matter and it is only by contorted manipulations that one can be provided. An alternative was to assume that market participants were optimizing agents in a competitive, equilibrium environment. Lucas and I achieved an interesting and powerful explanation of these related phenomena by studying household decision-making in a multi-period context.[1] What emerged was the Lucas – Rapping supply curve, which is now referred to in the literature as the Lucas supply curve.

The business cycle (or Phillips curve) implied by the Lucas–Rapping supply curve was driven by two behaviourial propositions. First, the suppliers of labour in making their labour – leisure choices on overtime, school attendance, labour force participation, overtime, full-time/part-time work, and retirement do so with respect to the trade-off between leisure and consumption today as well as leisure and consumption tomorrow. Under these circumstances, the supply of labour depends on the expected real interest rate. Secondly, if expectations on future prices are formed as a distributed lag on past prices, then the current supply of labour is dependent on the actual rate of inflation. However, this relationship is transient. In the long run, the supply of labour, for a given population, is independent of the inflation rate. This model rationalized the stagflation problem of the 1970s in terms of adapting expectations.

At a later point Professor Lucas, operating in the Walras – Fisher – Friedman tradition, combined rational expectations and monetarism with an equilibrium macroeconomic model. In general, the theory of rational expectations provides important insights into the way in which the future is impounded in the present. But the issue of concern here is its usefulness in explaining the business cycle, not its general usefulness.

Lucas's analysis is always clever and often brilliant, but in my judgement, this expectations assumption assumes away a monetary or, more generally, a demand-led business cycle, and in this sense it gives up too much for logical consistency. Surprise increases in demand that are expected to persist cannot lead to even a short-run change in output based on labour supply decisions. On the other hand, surprise-demand increases that are viewed as temporary can affect output, but only for a very short time. The investment process does not rescue this situation. Output is anchored at its Walrasian equilibrium level.[2]

The rational expectations assumption also eliminates even the temporary effectiveness of systematic monetary policy. In this respect, it leads to the same conclusions that Professor Friedman had reached in the 1950s. An activist monetary – fiscal policy is at best ineffective, at worst, destablilizing. The best monetary – fiscal policy is one based on steady, predictable rules.

In the final analysis, macro-models based on rational expectations provide a justification for an unregulated market economy with a minimum of discretion for the monetary and fiscal authorities. It is an analysis relevant for the debate on social organization, not economic policy in the more narrow sense of that term. Indeed, in a world with rational expectations, there is no room for activist monetary and fiscal policy, for there is really no demand-led business cycle, only a supply-led cycle or a random movement in prices and quantities.

More recently, Lucas' colleagues have promoted the idea that the business cycle is an equilibrium and supply-led phenomenon. Variations in the rate of growth in the labour force and technology generate a cycle in the sense of a systematic relationship between output and prices. It is in the spirit of this development that a deregulation or 'live and let live' literature has developed.

Of particular interest in this regard is the view that the level of output and prices not only is impervious to monetary and fiscal policy, but it is impervious as well to the deposit-creating activities of private banks. For them, banking, not unlike cosmetology, is just another service industry. Monetarism as espoused by Karl Brunner, Milton Friedman, the late Harry Johnson and the late Henry Simons is in conflict with this idea. I find it an unfortunate and even dangerous development. Debt deflation, to borrow a term from Irving Fisher, is an ever present threat in the current financial situation. Only by carefully monitoring and regulating this situation can the monetary and fiscal authorities hope to defuse this time-bomb.

My own interest in these questions had subsided by the late 1960s. I became more interested in the issues raised by the Vietnam War. I became involved in the anti-war movement. My general perspective became more international and my macroeconomic interests turned to secular, not business cycle matters.

At Chicago, students were sensitized to empirical reality. I was systematically trained in applied economotrics by H. Gregg Lewis who himself had been reared in the Chicago econometrics tradition as a student of Paul Douglas. I learned that there is an objective truth which is discoverable by hard thinking and observation. Of course the observer affects the observed, but in many instances the importance of this bias is easily overstated. In any event, I was taught that evidence, not emotion, friendship or personal profit, should determine an economist's position on issues. Since new evidence constantly accumulates, the economist must often alter his position on economic issues.

Changing your mind in favour of an unpopular idea can be economically and personally costly. The calculating thinker who wants to be rewarded for an idea, keeps it just one step ahead of the group's thinking. In this sense, socially successful thinkers are like politicians – they only flourish when they say what everyone wants to hear. Aside from the fact that you are financially penalized for changing your mind in favour of an unpopular idea, there is an emotional and intellectual cost.

Changing your mind and exploring new ideas requires that you go back to the beginning of the intellectual learning curve. This is personally costly, for there is no way to short-circuit this time-consuming process. And, there are other costs as well. People are understandably suspicious when you change your mind. Your credibility declines and you don't appear smart when you're not repeating catechisms.

My moral decision to participate in the anti-war movement was rooted in my experiences as a young boy. As a child, I knew a lot about American history. I was fascinated and inspired by colonial history and the early years of the American nation. Men like Jefferson, Hamilton and Madison were my heroes. The stress in my reading and thinking was on personal freedom, the right of self-determination, and the right to speak the truth as one sees it.

The soundness of these principles was reinforced by the attacks on personal freedom in Germany and the Soviet Union in the 1930s. The war solidified my ideas on personal freedom. It was a righteous struggle against totalitarian states. It was a great victory that America and its allies won against Germany and Japan. Enthusiasm for this victory combined with my admiration for the United States encouraged my faith in America. I learned patriotism, love of country and respect for the principles of democratic government.

But as the stories of the Old Testament instruct us, life is a continuous struggle between right and wrong. There is a necessary ebb and flow in the history of individuals as well as nations on this matter. The Holocaust imprinted on my mind the substantive nature of evil. But a somewhat less clear imprint also existed. I have always been interested in the North American Indians, a people whose history was quite familiar to me when I was growing up. I admired the heroic and ultimately unsuccessful efforts by King Philip in the east, Tecumsech in the midwest, Sitting Bull in the west and Geronimo in the southwest to stop the encroachment on their land by the white man. I felt a great injustice had been done to these people and it had been done by the very people who I admired for creating the nation. I was quite aware of the moral contradictions in every nation's history, and I could not in good conscience accept all of the actions of my government, especially when it was top dog.

I sought the reasons for American involvement in Vietnam by

examining the literature on imperialism. However, the essence of this literature is that the dominant nation materially gains from its actions. The cost of the US defence system in the post-war years far exceeded any gains to be achieved through exploitative trading prices or outright theft. Hobson had reached this conclusion for Great Britain at the time of the Boer War. It was still appropriate for the United States at the time of the Vietnam War.

I turned instead to a different set of ideas which better explained the American situation in the 1970s than the ideas on imperialism. In time I concluded that American action in Vietnam was, in a broad sense, an erroneous response to Soviet ambitions. Given American's role in ordering and managing an interrelated global economy, some catastrophic action was likely, for the leader's position is inevitably challenged. As it turned out, Vietnam was the wrong place for America to take a stand against encroachments on its international military and political authority.

The leadership role had been fulfilled by Great Britain in the years before World War I. War and industrial decline weakened the ability and resolve of the British to continue in this position. The role therefore went unfilled in the interwar years. It was inherited by the United States after World War II. Since the early 1970s the United States has had increasing difficulty in fulfilling its responsibilities as leader.

I became convinced of this position by the surprisingly rapid decline in the American economic, political and military position in the 1970s. The global economy was without a manager. Instead it was dependent on the workings of a decentralized market. Public lending was replaced by private lending, managed exchange rates were replaced by unstable market rates, predictable energy prices were replaced by gyrations in the price of oil, international macro-economic cooperation was replaced by uncoordinated actions, and a stable fiscal authority and a purposeful monetary authority were replaced by confusion and weakness. Both abroad and at home, the economy was without direction and leadership.

It is in this context that these essays were written. They are about the current effort of the United States to reposition itself in the new global order that is emerging.

NOTE

1. For an interesting perspective on this interaction, see Klamer.
2. This point has been noted by Okun among others.

REFERENCES

Friedman, Milton. *Essays in Positive Economics* (Chicago: University of Chicago Press, 1956).

Klamer, Arjo. *Conversations with Economists* (Totowa, NJ: Rowman and Allenheld, 1983) and published under the title, *The New Classical Macroeconomics* (Sussex: Wheatsheaf Books, 1984).

Lucas, Robert E. *Studies in Business Cycle Theory* (Cambridge, Mass.: 1981).

Okun, A. M. 'Rational expectations—with misperceptions as a theory of the business cycle,' *Journal of Money, Credit and Banking*, Part 2, November, 1980.

Simon, Herbert A. *Administrative Behavior*, revised second edition (New York: Free Press, 1976).

Acknowledgements

I would like to acknowledge those people who have influenced my thinking on many of the problems addressed in these essays.

At Chicago, H. G. Lewis, my thesis advisor and teacher in labour economics, taught me to respect the truth and to treat data and evidence with the care they deserve.

Herbert Simon, a long-time colleague at Carnegie-Mellon, gave me the rare experience of interacting with a man whose profound insights into economics, psychology, political science, philosophy, computers, technology and people have enriched my life and continue to inform my thinking in subtle and numerous ways.

Charles Kindleberger, a friend and colleague of recent years, reignited my interest in economic history and provided me with a context for understanding the current global political and economic situation.

David Bennett, a personal friend who, like myself, was imbued with the scholarly excitement at the University of Chicago in the 1950s, has been a source of ideas and encouragement during my work on these essays. I thank him for his patience, his extensive knowledge of history, his clarity of thought, and, most importantly, his wisdom and friendship.

Finally, I thank my wife, Judith, who has patiently stayed up into the late hours of the night to listen to every argument in the book. Her intelligence, her Methodist upbringing and her emotional steadiness and good humour have inspired me to push forward.

Waltham, Massachusetts April, 1988.

Part I
Deficits, Technology and Market Organization:
America's Economic Problems and Solutions

Introduction

The economic problems of the American economy contain both structural and cyclical components. The budget and trade deficits are the most prominent of these problems. The first essay in this part considers the political and economic forces behind these deficits, the prospects for eliminating them by public intervention, and the actions required to achieve their elimination. This includes changes in tax and expenditure policies, variation in dollar exchange rates, protectionism, cyclical adjustments in output in the United States and abroad, and technological change.

These essays also address the problems arising from the poor secular performance of productivity and the corresponding secular stagnation in real wages. Recognizing that the problem of real wage stagnation and trade deficits are in large part a reflection of the productivity problem, three of these essays address the issues raised by the productivity slowdown: workplace organization, worker motivation and training, technological change and industrial policies.

Much of my thinking on budget and trade deficits as well as technology has been influenced by my experiences in Washington DC. In 1980 I worked on public policy issues revolving around the deregulation of railroads. During the same time I served as a member of the economic advisory subcommittee of the Progressive Alliance, a group politically concerned with the decline of economic regulation. Between 1981 and 1985 I frequently lectured and participated in discussions at such diverse places as the Overseas Development Council, the Carnegie Foundation for Peace, the Public Interest Economics Centre, the National Science Foundation, American University and the Institute for Policy Studies.

In 1985 and 1986 I spent ten months at the National Academy of Sciences where I directed a study on technology and employment. This work gave me a chance to meet and exchange ideas with many scientists, engineers, businessmen and labour leaders. It also gave me an opportunity to tour many manufacturing and research facilities around the country.

The papers on bureaucracy, and productivity and technology were presented at Brandeis University, Cornell University, the University of Nôtre Dame, the University of California at Santa Cruz and Stanford University.

1 America's Budget and Trade Deficits*

INTRODUCTION

The US has two historically unprecedented deficits, its trade deficit and its budget deficit. In 1986 the trade deficit was approximately $147 billion a year, or $1700 per family. The budget deficit was over $200 billion a year, or about 5.2 per cent of the Gross National Product. These deficits have been cited as evidence that the United States is on a consumption binge. In actuality the United States has financed a large increase in government spending on both the aged and the military without restricting private consumption or investment. Indeed, investment as a percentage of GNP remains high by post-World War II standards. With foreign indulgence, the United States has borrowed from abroad.

Following the recent plunge of world stock markets, there has been renewed stress on the position that trade and budget deficits have the potential to destabilize international exchange rates, domestic interest rates and financial markets generally. In a more optimistic and equally overstated argument, the trade deficit is financed by foreigners who willingly accumulate dollars, a process not likely to abort, or at least no more likely to abort than if it were Americans accumulating dollars, while the budget deficit is either too small to warrant anxiety, or regardless of its size, simply does not matter. Neither position is fully convincing. These are all extreme views on deficit problems. The deficits are not benign but they are not the end of the world either.

---

*Written in the spring of 1987 and revised in the autumn of that year.

The Burden of Trade Deficits

The trade deficit has both a cyclical and secular component. It developed in the late 1960s and showed clear signs of trending upwards during the 1970s. It mushroomed in the 1980s. While the trade deficits will create economic problems for future generations, matters are less certain with regard to the budget deficit. The trade deficit, and its reflection, borrowing from abroad, will eventually require repayment in the form of goods sent abroad. About 85 per cent of American imports are consumer goods and will not generate the future production necessary to repay the foreign loans which financed their purchase. This is the real impact of the trade deficit on future generations, and it is a large and growing one. It cannot easily be ignored.

Any attempt by the United States to avoid repayment by using its reserve currency status to inflate away its international debt would be frustrated by the short-term nature of much of the debt, and by the fact that such an effort would so fundamentally destabilize the world trading system as to yield America only a pyrrhic victory. By the same token, it would destroy global confidence if the United States behaved like its Latin American creditors and defaulted on its debts.

The Burden of the Budget Deficit

The budget deficit has both cyclical and secular components. It has been large and growing since the early 1970s and in the early 1980s it increased several fold. The burden of this cyclical and secular deficit is much more difficult to assess than that of the trade deficit. As long as the budget deficit contributes to expanded output, there is no burden. Quite the contrary, the deficit is an economic blessing. Remember the anxious summer of 1982, when falling employment, unstable financial markets, and the Third World debt crisis placed the world economy on the brink of depression. The American budget deficit prevented a potential disaster by providing the world economy with Keynesian stimulus.

In this scenario, the continuing budget deficit can threaten either eventual recession if it is precipitously reduced by government tax or expenditure action at a time of falling private spending or inflation if it is monetized at a time of rising private spending. At the present time, the inflationary potential is less real than the recessionary potential.

Among other things, America's peacetime inflations have been driven by cost factors, not budget deficits. The unprecedented peacetime inflation of the 1970s was clearly the result of the 1973 and 1979 oil price shocks, not excessive budget deficits. Indeed, the sharp increase in budget deficits in the 1980s has been associated with falling, not rising inflation rates.

This is not to imply that budget deficits, or indeed, corporate or consumer deficits, are never the cause of inflation. Sometimes they are. However, even though today's budget deficits are larger than they were in the 1970s, they are still small compared to budget deficits in countries that have had or have highly inflationary situations. During Israel's inflationary experiences of the mid-1980s its budget deficit relative to GNP was 17 per cent, while inflationary Brazil and Argentina had ratios that were 10 to 27 per cent and 15 per cent respectively.

Sargent has argued that it is government net interest payments as a per cent of total government expenditures, not the ratio of the deficit to GNP, that is the relevant statistic for judging the inflationary potential of deficit spending. In the 1980s, both rapidly growing deficits and rising real interest rates caused a significant increase in the share of government outlays devoted to interest payments on the national debt. Between 1979 and 1987, interest payments went from about 8 per cent of total outlays to about 14 per cent. It is of interest to note that despite the fact that the ratio of debt to GNP was very high at the end of World War II, interest payments were only 5 per cent of government outlays. Recall, however, that the effect on government interest obligations of the large outstanding debt was more than offset by interest rates kept low by government financial market regulation.

A continuously rising government debt to GNP ratio, coupled with high or rising interest rates, does invite a debt crisis in the sense that government interest obligations either crowd out other government programmes and outlays, or provoke a taxpayer's revolt or create resistance on the part of government bond holders. In response, the government might be inspired to finance its outlays by resort to the printing press. The Western European governments did it after World War I and the Latin American governments do it today. However, the United States is not a war-torn economy nor is its political system as vulnerable and weak as many of those in Latin America. Expenditure reductions and tax increases remain painful but real political options.[1]

But it is not the threat of inflation or recession that is usually meant by the suggestion that a continuing budget deficit imposes a burden on future generations. The claim that there is a burden applies to budget deficits that continue throughout all stages of the business cycle and are permanently enshrined in the macroeconomic landscape of a nation. There is certainly a secular as well as cyclical component to the American budget deficits.

If a structural or secular deficit in some way encourages current consumption at the expense of investment, then future consumption is compromised by deficit spending. In this sense, deficits can burden future generations. Solow and Blinder argue that under conditions of full employment, bond-financed deficits stimulate private consumption while Buchanan contends that it is public spending and public consumption that is encouraged. Tax increases would reduce either private consumption or public spending. The positions of Solow-Blinder and Buchanan imply that deficit financing by the current generation proceeds without regard to the tax burden that is being imposed on their children. The tax liability placed on future generations is not a matter of special concern to the current generation.

Barro has developed a contrary position. He contends that people are concerned about future generations and that they will be indifferent between taxes today and properly discounted taxes tomorrow. They see themselves and their children as one. Savings, not consumption, vary with current taxes. A tax increase designed to reduce a current budget deficit will reduce after-tax savings and have no effect on either consumption or investment. Deficits impose no burden on future generations.

As a practical matter I would reject this view sometimes called the Ricardo Equivalence Theorem. People are myopic and at full employment, tax-financed spending, as opposed to deficit spending, accommodates investment at the expense of consumption. However, I am uncomfortable with the argument that it is changes in the real interest rate that stimulates investment. After all, lower interest rates can crowd in consumption as well as investment borrowing. Moreover, except for housing, investment is not reliably sensive to the interest rate. In any event, the exact form of the taxes being considered is crucial. An income tax is more likely to contain consumption than a tax on corporate profits. In summary then, eliminating budget deficits by raising taxes will probably moderate consumption and encourage investment but the effect might be rather modest.

With trade deficits imposing burdens on future generations and with budget deficits having similar but less pronounced effects, both deficits should be reduced. However, a tax increase in the United States will not automatically reduce imports and at full employment its effect on constraining consumption might be rather modest. On the other hand, it might result in recession. Under these circumstances only by reducing purchasing power will it reduce the trade deficit. In this event, investment would fall, not rise. It is a very subtle matter to eliminate budget deficits without depressing the economy. Timing is crucial. Yet in a highly politicized system such as the United States, duress determines the timing of tax changes. Well-timed tax changes rarely occur.

A Deeper Problem with Continuing Deficits

These are the economic problems with the current deficits for future generations. But perhaps more disturbing is the continuation of both deficits in the face of underlying economic and political problems in the United States. The trade deficit reflects a decline in American technological superiority as well as an inability of the United States and its trading partners to coordinate global economic policy with respect to trade, finance, international debt and domestic macroeconomic policy. The budget deficit reflects domestic political disarticulation. Both developments weaken the Western Alliance and America's leadership role in international policy formation. They undermine the development of reasonable economic policy just as seriously today as in the early 1930s. It is politics, not economics, that is the great threat to world economic stability.

Reducing the Deficits

Eventually, these deficits must be reduced, although a solution can probably be delayed for a while longer. When these imbalances are eventually addressed, specific changes will be necessary. The elimination of the budget deficit requires either an increase in taxes – currently political anathema in the United States – or a reduction in the $400 billion a year of financial assistance to the aged, veterans and welfare recipients – a proposal not yet politically popular – or a reduction in the $300 billion a year military budget – a move that is attracting some popular support after a long, seven-year military build-up and after the defence-oriented Reagan administration cut the ground from under its own feet by selling arms to the Iranians.

There are several ways to reduce the trade deficit. Currency depreciation eventually works if it occurs in large enough doses. Unfortunately, the process of adjusting prices is often halting and slow. Over the the past three years, the 40 per cent decline in the exchange value of the dollar against the yen and mark has not affected the dollar value of American imports and has had only a small effect on the dollar value of exports. In real terms, imports have not been contained although exports have begun to grow. Apparently, a 40 per cent depreciation of the dollar is not a large enough dose!

Effective protectionist action can block imports, although it can also balkanize the world economy. In this regard, the current restrictionist posture of Congress is much overstated. The current trade proposals of Congress consist mostly of public relations and electoral posturing. In the final analysis they leave a great deal of discretion to the Executive branch which has been, is, and will remain a bastion of free trade regardless of who is in power. Heavily influenced by strong anti-protectionist forces on Wall Street and American export industries, the possibilities of retaliation by foreign governments, and relatively low unemployment rates, it is unlikely that virulent protectionism will prevail.

Some combination of an American recession and a Western European and Japanese expansion could reduce the trade deficit. Presently, there is no mention of purposely slowing the American economy and there are no clear signals that the private decision-making process will soon abort the current six-year expansion. Similarly, neither the Japanese nor the Western Europeans seem inclined to absorb large quantities of American goods, especially if the price for Japan will be undesired changes in domestic consumption patterns, and for Western Europe inflation or increases in budget deficits as a per cent of GNP.

Finally, there is a structural element in the trade deficit that cannot be eliminated without a basic improvement in the process of finding and introducing new production technologies and new products into the economy. America has a competitiveness problem due to eroding technological superiority.

THE US BUDGET DEFICIT

The US budget deficit is at the centre of the debate on domestic and world macroeconomic policy. This deficit has been large since 1975 and has been growing rapidly since 1981. It has been blamed for the appreciation of the dollar between 1980 and the autumn of 1985, about 100 per cent against the mark and the yen. It has also been blamed for the large and growing US trade deficit. And last, but by no means least important, it has been blamed for the high inflation corrected 'real' interest rates in the 1980s, averaging about 5 per cent compared to a post-World War II average of about 1 per cent.

The Budget Deficit and Dollar Appreciation
The budget deficit is not responsible for the appreciation of the dollar from 1980 to 1985. This is now apparent after the dollar

depreciated massively in 1986 and 1987 despite continuing high budget deficits. A view somewhat less comfortable for those who promote unregulated international financial markets is that excessive foreign exchange rate variations result from speculative activity and only weakly relate to interest rate changes, inflation rate changes or other variables which reflect underlying economic fundamentals. The same speculative forces that buffet world stockmarkets, buffet the foreign exchange market. The exchange rate is a speculative variable, not unlike the price of common stocks.[2]

The Budget Deficit and Real Interest Rates

Despite the fact that the supply of new bonds to the financial markets measures only 2 per cent of the stock of existing bonds, there is a rather popular argument that the budget deficit raises interest rates as the government attempts to induce the market to absorb its paper. This is an uninteresting argument.

A different and more interesting argument for why budget deficits raise interest rates is articulated clearly by Tobin. He along with many other economists assert that the mix of monetary and fiscal policy is distorted by abnormally large budget deficits. Here it is argued that for the past seven years, the Federal Reserve Bank has been forced by budget deficits running about 5 per cent of GNP to drive the real interest rate to about 5 per cent, an action necessary to restrain overexuberant demand. In earlier years, budget deficits of 1 per cent of GNP permitted interest rates of comparable magnitude.

I have reservations about this argument. The interest rate is an expectational variable best influenced or controlled by the manipulation of market expectations.[3] Bennett, Pulley and I have argued elsewhere that during the period under consideration the Federal Reserve Bank probably has not had sufficient authority and power to reliably or significantly influence the market's expectations.[4] More promising is the view that high interest rates are a market phenomenon resulting from the necessity of paying high rates to people in order to induce them to hold bonds when speculation in competing assets is rampant. Speculative exhilaration in common stocks, real estate and foreign exchange creates the expectation of high real returns on these assets and corresponding high returns are required on assets like bonds.

These comments do not dispose of the argument that high interest rates might be caused by current budget deficits because they are a harbinger of future inflation. Aside from the statistical difficulty of establishing this proposition, recall that it has been already mentioned, the American deficits are relatively small and, moreover, it is very uncertain whether the printing press as opposed to tax increases will be the chosen instrument of taxation when the deficit is finally reduced.

The Budget Deficit and The Trade Deficit

The budget deficits do, however, contribute to the trade deficits. The American budget deficits of the 1980s have been active, stimulatory deficits reflecting the very large personal and corporate tax cuts of 1981 as well as the large increases in government military expenditures during the decade. Personal taxes were cut by about 17 per cent between 1981 and 1983, corporate taxes fell from 4 per cent of corporate profits in 1980 to 2.5 per cent in 1985, and defence spending rose from 5 per cent of GNP in 1980 to 7 per cent in 1985. The budget deficits have averaged 4.6 per cent of GNP between 1981 and 1986. However, when state government surpluses are included, the average for this statistic is 2.9 per cent. Nevertheless, the US was actively expanding income and purchasing power, and hence stimulating import demand.

Although many of the Western European governments have had larger deficits as a percentage of GNP than the United States, their deficits are in most instances the passive result of their recessions – falling tax receipts and rising recession-related expenditures – not an active result of government efforts to stimulate the economies. And, not only have the Western Europeans been less expansionary compared to the US, but also compared to their own policies in the late 1970s. Indeed, in West Germany and Japan fiscal policy has been assiduously contractive. These policies discourage imports by restraining world economic expansion.

Historical Background for American Budget Policy

American macroeconomic policy in 1981 was driven by political and military considerations. The public, angry with inflation and confronted with stagnating real wages, wanted the unreconcilable – lower taxes, improved government services, smaller budget deficits and limits to the growth of government. The Reagan administration wanted to get 'government off our backs', which sounded a lot like balanced budgets and lower spending. Their actual macroeconomic programme was to increase defence spending – an attempt to project American power – and to cut taxes – an attempt to satisfy both their own anti-government ideology and the popular demand for tax relief, a demand born of the inflation in the 1970s. Compensating reductions in other government programmes were never seriously proposed. It was politically too hazardous to recommend large reductions in the numerous entitlement programmes, the only programmes where significant reductions were technically possible.

The 1981 fiscal programme implied large deficits and an increase in the relative size of government. There is some irony in the fact that it was the societies of Western Europe where social democratic influence is strong, and not the individualistic, 'cowboy' society of the United States, that actually introduced fiscal restraint.

That the programme was contradictory did not escape notice, but logic was not the overriding concern in the first year of the Reagan *blitzkrieg*. Supply-siders alleged that output growth would generate tax receipts sufficient to balance the budget. Other administration supporters felt that tax cuts and the resulting deficits would force government spending cuts in social services. But both hopes proved fanciful. The result of the 1981 decisions was a series of very large budget deficits.[5]

And the budget deficit is still the major macroeconomic issue in the current political debate. There is now popular concern over the deficit. But because it has proven impossible to form a broad coalition around either tax increases, reductions in entitlements, or reductions in military spending, the deficit persists. Some holdouts notwithstanding, most economists and politicians think the budget deficit is an actual or potential problem. The prevailing opinion did not, however, facilitate a Democratic win in the 1984 election on the budget issue, and it may not be a rallying point in future elections.

The standard association of large deficits with inflation, appears not immediately relevant to the current situation in the United States. Quite the contrary, the large and rising deficits have been associated with disinflation. The inflation rate was 8.9 per cent in 1981. It fell to 1.1 per cent in 1986. Oil prices have fallen because of low demand due to slow, world-wide economic growth and rapidly falling oil use per unit of GNP. The 'reserve army' of oil, as it were, broke the back of OPEC. Meanwhile, money wages have grown slowly. The recession of 1981–1982 in the US created a large pool of unemployed labour which is only now being depleted. The US unemployment rate rose to over 10 per cent in late 1982. By the autumn of 1987 it had fallen to below 6 per cent.

The American budget deficit has provided the United States as well as the world economy with Keynesian stimulus. In doing so, massive quantities of imports have been attracted to the United States and this has left the American people with a large international debt combined with import dependency. With the

American economy near or at full employment, imports are necessary to sustain current levels of government purchases, private consumption and private investment. But the trade deficit cannot help to maintain the American standard of living indefinitely. Like any other debtor, the United States is politically weakened in the international arena by its debtor status. Meanwhile, the debt imposes a burden on future American generations.

THE US TRADE DEFICIT

Historical Considerations

In the long period of American industrial growth from the early nineteenth century to the years just prior to World War II, the American market was a protected market. Despite a long and politically difficult struggle, American manufacturers in the East who needed protection from inexpensive British goods, defeated the free trade position of American farmers in the South and West. The American market was successfully insulated from foreign competition during the entire nineteenth century and the early part of the twentieth century. Even after the Armistice of 1918 by which time the US had become an international creditor and its industry highly competitive, protectionist policies prevailed. America's isolationism was reflected fully in the Fordney – McCumber Tariff Act of 1922 and the Hawley – Smoot Tariff Act 1929.

America emerged from World War II with extraordinary economic capability. Unlike Germany and Japan where plant and equipment were destroyed both by Allied air attacks and land invasions, the US productive capability was increased and modernized by a wartime investment programme. More plant and equipment were put in place in the first three years of the war than during the seven-year investment boom of the 1920s. With industrial dominance, the US accepted military, financial and industrial leadership. To serve this role it was necessary for the United States to open its financial and commodity markets by a commitment to the integrative potential of free trade.

Before the war, American manufacturing exports were never more than 5 per cent of its manufacturing output. But after the war international trade became increasingly important to the United States. In 1960, the United States exported 9 per cent of its manufacturing output. By 1980 this figure had grown to 25 per cent. However, because economic conditions were depressed abroad since the early 1980s, American exports as a share of domestic manufacturing output fell to 18 per cent by 1985. These figures do not include the sales of American affiliates in Mexico, Taiwan and elsewhere, and for this reason they are more relevant to a discussion of employment than of corporate profits.

In the manufacturing sector, the US is increasingly specialized in the export of technologically sophisticated products. Of total manufacturing exports in 1985, 42 per cent were high-technology products, defined as products in which research and development costs are high. About three-quarters of the high-technology exports consisted of communications equipment, electrical components, computers, aircraft and aircraft parts, and professional and scientific instruments. The remaining quarter were plastics and resins, drugs, industrial chemicals, engines and turbines, missiles and ordinance.

Of total American goods exported in 1985, manufactured goods consisted of 76 per cent, the remainder being mostly agricultural products, minerals and fuels. Agricultural products as a share of total commodity exports has fallen throughout the post-war period. In the expansionary years 1965–69, this share was 25 per cent. In the recovery years 1976–79, 20 per cent. In the globally stagnant year of 1985 it had fallen to about 14 per cent. As the world economy's capability to produce food has increased, the US exports have become more concentrated in manufacturing exports.

Between 1946 and 1971 the US ran export surpluses on merchandise account, including exports of manufactured goods, raw materials and agricultural commodities. These surpluses were declining in the post-war period, and since 1976, the merchandise account has been continuously in deficit. This deficit grew rapidly in the 1980s. However, because of earnings from invisibles (service exports and income from real and financial assets overseas), the current account deficits were relatively small in the late 1970s. Starting in 1983, however, the current account deficits became large. The US became a large net overseas borrower and is now about $200 billion in debt. This debt is growing at the rate of well over $100 billion a year.

This growing international debt is widely seen as a problem for the United States because it must eventually be repaid with exports and because foreigners, not to mention American multinationals, might at some point flee dollar-denominated assets, plunging the dollar downwards. However, Americans are also likely to flee the dollar. In this regard, foreign-owned dollar assets do not raise any special problems unless there is a very strong home currency preference or unless governments force their investors to behave in concert for political or military reasons.

Furthermore, if foreigners are willing to have their dollar assets accumulate, the US simply exports stocks, bonds and real estate in exchange for consumption and capital goods. In this instance, there is no repatriation problem. There is, however, a concern when foreign ownership of real and paper assets grows as a percentage of total domestic real and paper assets. This concern partly reflects the perceived loss of international influence. But there is also an uneasiness that foreigners will control too much of American industry and have too much influence on American politics. In an important sense the problem with a continuous, large trade deficit is that we must either trade future goods for present goods or present political influence for present goods.

Some Facts on the US Trade Deficit

Let us consider the trade deficit more closely. American merchandise trade between the years 1980 and 1986 reflects the sharp economic decline of 1981 – 82 and the subsequent expansion in the US, coupled with stagnation abroad. From the beginning to the end of this six-year period the dollar value of American exports hardly changed whilst the real quantity actually fell. The dollar value of American exports to Western Europe declined. The OPEC countries and most of Latin America also reduced their purchases from the United States. Exports to Japan and the Asian rim grew slowly.

At the same time, the dollar value (and real quantity) of American imports rose dramatically from everywhere except the OPEC countries, where falling oil prices reduced the cost of imported oil. As a result of stagnating exports and exploding imports a massive American trade deficit erupted. The American trade balance went from a manageable deficit of about $25 billion in 1980 – manageable in the sense that earnings on invisibles were large enough to finance this deficit – to an extraordinary deficit in 1986 of about $150 billion – a deficit which exceeded net earnings on invisibles by $114 billion.

These findings do not change in implication if real as opposed to nominal trade deficits are measured, nor were the results significantly altered by the end of 1987. The rise in the real deficit was arrested by the end of 1986, but the nominal deficit continued to grow. It is estimated that this deficit will be about $170 billion by the end of 1987.

There are several explanations for the dreary performance of American exports. Agricultural exports fell in nominal dollar value from 42 billion in 1980 to 30 billion in 1985. This poor performance was because of increased world-wide self-sufficiency in agricultural production and because of the low rate of income growth abroad. In the 1970s food consumption abroad grew by 34 million tons per year while the average annual increase in grain production abroad was only 24 million tons. In the 1980s, on the other hand, foreign consumption grew by only 19 million tons a year while foreign grain output increased by 29 million tons a year – a development which partly reflects Western European farm subsidies. Western Europe turned from a net grain importer to a net exporter between the 1970s and 1980s. Continued Japanese food import restraints also contributed to the poor American export performance.

The unexpected and extraordinary rise in the exchange value of the dollar between 1982 and 1985 was not an especially important factor in the decline of American agricultural exports. Among other reasons, the dollar did not rise against the currencies of important competitive grain exporters like Argentina, Canada and Australia. Moreover, an increased cost of imports would not deter imports that were excluded by protective barriers. In addition, if the phenomenal rise in the dollar between 1982 and 1985 had had an important role in discouraging American agricultural exports, then its equally precipitous decline since late 1985 should have substantially stimulated American agricultural exports, which it has not. It would appear that the changing exchange value of the dollar is only of secondary importance in explaining the behaviour of American agricultural exports.

The poor performance of manufacturing exports to Western Europe reflects the weak European recovery following the severe recession in the early 1980s. The weakness of this recovery is seen in the Western European unemployment statistics. Averaged across countries, this rate has remained above 10 per cent since late 1982, when the American recovery began. Unemployment rates at this level had not previously been seen in Western Europe since the interwar years.

The decline in American exports to many Third World countries, especially those in Latin America, resulted from the combination of their staggering foreign debts and their own very depressed economic conditions since 1982. They were heavily in debt to the Western banks – mainly American – because oil money was lent to them to finance American and other imports in the 1970s. Their credit deteriorated under the weight of these large debts. They could not continue to borrow to finance the purchase of American products. Indeed, they were driven by their debtor status not only to reduce imports but to increase exports.

Finally, except in the case of some foodstuffs and raw materials, American exporters have been unable to crack the inwardness of the Japanese market, and the last six years have been no exception to this ongoing problem.

The dollar value of American imports increased greatly from all over the world between 1980 and 1986. While this might to some limited extent be explained by the rise in the exchange value of the American dollar which caused a fall in import prices and a rise in export prices as exchange rate variation was passed through to import and export prices, it is more likely the result of a rather strong recovery in the US with its attendant rise in American income. With an increased ability to pay, there was an unusually high increase in American demand for everything: automobiles, construction machinery, machine tools, electrical components, and consumer electronic goods from Japan; electrical components and consumer goods from South Korea, Taiwan and other countries on the Asian rim; raw materials, natural gas and automobiles from Canada; raw materials and agricultural products from Africa and Latin America; communications equipment, machine tools, textile machinery, autos and foodstuffs from Western Europe; and oil from the Middle East.

AMERICAN COMPETITIVENESS

The trade deficit has prompted a Presidential Commission, many government reports, and several private studies bemoaning the decline in American 'competitiveness'. There are several senses in which a country can become less competitive and the policy actions required depend on the source of the problem.

Real Factors
If for some standard commodities – steel, autos, wheat or farm machinery – output per unit of labour input (or per some combined input measure) rises more slowly at home than abroad, then the country is losing real competitiveness in the sense that its exports embody increasingly more combined inputs than its imports. This might be termed a decline in real competitiveness. In this sense the United States became gradually less competitive throughout the entire post-World War II period as Western Europe and Japan first recovered from the war, and then introduced superior production methods in the manufacture of standard goods. These effects on the competitiveness of American industry were extended by the rise of

the newly industrializing economies of the Asian rim in the 1970s.

But this process of increasing foreign productivity has been continuous and quantitatively significant throughout the post-war years, a growing advantage that was especially evident in the case of Japan. Indeed, while it continues into the 1980s, it does so at a decelerated rate. National differentials in the rate of productivity growth can account for the structural or long-term deterioration in the US trade balance, but not for the precipitous decline experienced since 1982.

Monetary Factors

A country can suffer a deteriorating trade balance because of monetary, rather than real events. A relative rise in its money wage rates – a change that often reflects domestic inflation – or an appreciation in its currency will tend to reduce the physical quantity of exports and increase the physical quantity of imports. Thus the trade-weighted doubling in the exchange value of the dollar from the winter of 1980 to the autumn of 1985 reduced American competitiveness in this sense. The appreciation of the dollar was caused by speculators, not by underlying market fundamentals. This process drove the price of the dollar up as expectations that the price of the dollar would rise caused it to rise. Neither changes in purchasing power parity nor interest rate differentials could account for this appreciation of the dollar.

If the physical quantity of both exports and imports are sensitive to the changing value of the dollar, then the US could suffer from a competitiveness problem, one caused by monetary, not real factors. However, import demand does not seem very sensitive to relative prices, and despite an over 40 per cent rise in the dollar against key currencies between 1980 and 1985, it would not appear that much of the trade deficit was caused by monetary factors. Perhaps as little as 20 per cent of the deficit can be explained by the appreciation of the dollar. This small percentage should not be surprising given the sluggish, uncertain effect of the dollar's decline which has followed its rise.

Income Factors

A third reason why a country might develop a trade deficit and decreased competitive ability is because of differential rates of income growth at home as compared to abroad, or because credit dries up to overseas importers who must borrow to buy. The effect of differential income growth rates depends on the sensitivity of import demand both at home and abroad. If these elasticities are high, then large changes in differential growth rates can create significant trade imbalances.

In both the European Community and developing countries, real income growth rates fell significantly relative to growth rates in the United States since the early 1980s. This can account for some of the American trade deficit. From past studies we know that the elasticity of import demand with respect to GNP is of the order of two. Assume world growth rates were about 2 percentage points per year higher for the past five years. This would increase US exports by 20 per cent or a total of about $40 billion, about one quarter of the trade deficit in 1987.

The Third World debt problem also contributed to the trade deficit. Credit-financed exports from the US, which were financed by the government in the 1950s and 1960s and then by private loans in the 1970s, were no longer possible. Perhaps as much as $20 billion in exports were lost due to this development.

Finally, we should keep in mind that the US personal savings rate fell from 6 per cent of disposable income to just over 3 per cent – about a $120 billion savings decline in 1986. Part of these funds was used to purchase imports: a conservative estimate would be about $20 billion. Thus, all three factors – income growth abroad, Third World debt and personal savings in the US – account for perhaps $80 billion of the $150 billion 1986 trade deficit, or about 55 per cent of the deficit. There remains a substantial structural deficit.

Technological Factors

In a dynamic, growing economy new products and new production methods are continuously being introduced. As these replace existing products and processes, exports are stimulated and imports are discouraged. An economy becomes less competitive when it does not push the technological frontier as fast as do its competitors. In technology, the US is losing its competitive edge, and this decline might not be properly indexed by standard productivity measures.

The current indexes of productivity measure only certain types of quality changes: those which are cost-related, like extras on automobiles or credit facilities at department stores. On the other hand, these indexes do not account for new products like video-recorders, nor do they account for quality changes that are not cost-related. Quality changes that are not cost-related include such things as an improvement in computer memory capacity, or the sound quality of a radio or TV set, or the reduction in the repair costs on consumer durables, or increases in the fuel efficiency of automobiles. Foreign productivity measures have similar limitations. Thus important elements of technological improvements are not covered by productivity measures. A country with well-behaved, measured productivity advances might be quite far behind in improving the quality of its old products or in introducing new products.

When the Japanese penetrated the American market with fuel-efficient cars (which also required less repairs than American cars), or with video-recorders – the two together amounted to about 30 billion a year in exports to the US – these gains were not signalled by their rapid productivity advance measured against the US. When we consider technology, we must move beyond standard measures. We shall see that the US does have a technology problem that might account for its structural trade deficit.

COMPETITION IN TECHNOLOGY

Between 1980 and 1986, the turnaround in the US trade deficit with the Europeans was 44 billion dollars, almost identical to the 43.5 billion turnaround with the Japanese. Yet, the American media, vibrating on the trade deficits, stressed the threat to American economic supremacy from Japan, not from West Germany, the strongest economy in Western Europe. If the only concern were the static employment effects of the deficit or its effect on shifting labour from high-wage manufacturing to low-wage services, there should be no distinction between the two nations. But there are other concerns and there are sound economic reasons why the attitude towards the Japanese differs from the attitude towards the Germans and their Common Market allies.

The US as an Exporter of High Technology Products
In a dynamic growth process, an industrial economy goes through several different stages of growth. These stages can be defined by the goods that are produced. In the early period of industrialization, economies concentrate on the production of textiles and clothing. In the next growth stage, industrialised countries concentrate on the production of metals, the fabrication and mass assembly of metal products like autos and ships, the assembly of a variety of non-metal products, and the advanced processing of goods. At an even more advanced stage, there is a gradual shift to increasing involvement in the production of high-technology products, which are defined by relative expenditures on research and development. This includes such products as electrical components, electrical

equipment, polymers, other chemicals, drugs, computers, scientific instruments, aircraft and parts, aerospace products, communications equipment and aircraft engines.

The United States is presently the most advanced of the high-technology economies. However, both the Germans and Japanese have rebuilt their post-war economies and they are now viable competitors of the United States in most 'old' and many 'high-technology' products. None the less, while the US has clearly lost its edge in steel, autos, many lines of machinery and other second-stage products, it remains dominant in many high-technology products.

In 1970, the US share of high-technology exports among six countries – the US, Canada, Japan, France, West Germany and Great Britain – was 36 per cent. In 1982 this figure stood at 33 per cent, a figure that indicates very little relative deterioration. But the Japanese share went from 14 per cent to 21 per cent, indicating that the American position had deteriorated *vis-à-vis* the Japanese. In recent years the results are somewhat more ambiguous. To consider the period 1982-86, we must examine a slighly different set of statistics.

The export of American high-technology products has been stagnant between 1982 and 1987, but high-technology product imports have risen rapidly during these years. In 1981, US high-technology exports exceeded high-technology imports by about $26 billion. By 1987 this surplus had fallen to zero. This does not ncessarily reflect a real deterioration in American competitiveness. With US income rising relative to the rest of the world, one would expect US imports of everything, including high-technology products, to rise compared to exports.

The high-technology trade balance is not a very good measure of the underlying competitive position of American industry unless growth among trading nations is balanced. A better measure is the American share of total world output in these products regardless of whether the products are exported or sold in the domestic market. On the basis of this statistic the US has not suffered unusually large losses in the 1980s, although its share of high-technology output among the leading six producers has declined.

A variety of broad indicators suggest that the US remains technologically dominant, but that its relative position has slipped, especially *vis-à-vis* the Japanese. In 1985, the US spent more on research and development than did Germany and Japan, although its lead has diminished, especially compared to Japan. If we exclude military R & D and compare only public and private nondefence expenditures, the US is still absolutely dominant, although the margin is much smaller because about 30 per cent of US R & D expenditures are for defence purposes. On the other hand, if we ignore military R & D and then measure relative positions, private and publically-sponsored non-military R & D is a smaller fraction of American GNP than it is for Germany or Japan.

The United States leads Japan and West Germany in the number of R & D engineers and scientists per civilian employee, although again, its lead has declined in the last fifteen years. The US has granted a constant number of patents to American inventors, while the number granted to foreign inventors has nearly trebled. However, the US retains an absolute advantage. On the other hand, there has been a sharp decline in the number of patent applications by Americans to foreign governments. Likewise, this is true for most major countries except Japan, which continues energetically to apply for patents abroad. The US has a commanding lead in the number of scientific and engineering publications and Nobel Prizes.

These rather broad indicators suggest that the US still has a leading position in technology, but that its lead has been diminishing over time. It is this *relative* decline that has raised great concern in the United States. There is special concern about the Japanese whose technical capabilities seem to be advancing most rapidly.

More on the US, Japan and Germany
Table 1. 1 shows some survey data which indicate the relative

Table 1.1 Assessment by chief executive officers of more than 200 European companies of the national ranking of high technology capability

Industry	United States	Japan	West Germany	Scan-dinavia	United Kingdom	France
Computing	1	2	3	4–5	6	4–5
Electronics	1–2	1–2	3	4	6–7	6–7
Telecommunications	1	2	3	4	5–6	5–6
Biotechnology	1	2	3	4	5	n.a.
Chemicals	1	2	3	4	5	6–7
Metals/Alloys	2	1	3	4	5–6	5–6
Engineering	1	2	3	4	5	6
Manufacturing	1–2	1–2	3	4	5	6
Robotics	2	1	3	4	5	5
Mean rank	1·3	1·7	3·0	4·2	5·4	5·8

Source: Taken directly from Kenneth Flamn, *Targeting the Computer*, p.4.

ranking of countries in the high-technology areas. We see that the US clearly ranks first in the minds of European CEO's with the Japanese second and the West Germans third. This rating is consistent with data on exports of high-technology products. In Table 1. 2 we see that the US has the highest percentage of exports in seven of the eleven commodity categories when compared to the exports of Japan, West Germany, France and the United Kingdom. The Japanese lead in three categories and the West Germans in one.

Table 1.2 Share of total world exports by leading country in selected technology-intensive products, 1984

Industry	Leading Nation	Share of Exports %
Aircraft and parts	USA	43
Chemicals	USA	22
Radio and receiving equipment	Japan	79
Office and computing equipment	USA	37
Electrical machinery and equipment	USA	22
Communications equipment	Japan	34
Professional and scientific equipment	Japan	30
Drugs	USA	18
Plastics and synthetics	Germany	20
Engines and turbines	USA	30
Agricultural chemicals	USA	33

Source: Kenneth Flamn, *Targeting the Computer,* p. 3.

American military and political leaders feel that American international power and prestige are partly rooted in technological leadership. Military leaders are particularly concerned that the loss of autarky in advanced technology weakens the US militarily. Moreover, without a monopoly at the technological frontier, the spread of advanced weapons in the international arena is difficult to control.

I think it proper to fear that trade adjustments necessitated by decline in American competitiveness in autos, steel and some machinery lines will be more difficult if the US suffers from a declining competitive position in high-technology goods as well. If the US does not continuously develop new products and processes and move down the learning curves, its high labour costs will force it to retreat from many industries and prevent it from entering new ones.

It is recognized, of course, that the Germans have an advanced chemical industry with competitive advantages in synthetics and plastics, a highly efficient machine tool industry, and an excellent medical and scientific instruments industry. They participate with other Western European countries in the production of the airbus, a strong competitor against American-made aircraft. It is also recognized that the European Space Agency's unmanned space launch capability has ended NASA's monopoly. However, unlike the Japanese, the Europeans do not have a very advanced computer industry and they are not competitors in microelectronic technologies. Moreover, Western Europe does not evidence the rapid technological advances in many other areas that Japan has achieved.

Japan as a Competitor in High Technology

The Japanese have built what Frank Gibney has called the world's first great unarmed economy. In only 35 years and without the benefit of colonies or raw materials, they have gone from an economy completely destroyed by war to the world's third largest economy. With great economic momentum, they have transited rapidly through each stage of industrial development and now are pushing the frontiers of technology. They have achieved this with highly motivated students who have learned the fundamentals of mathematics, science, history and language by the time they are eighteen, an achievement which shows up on international standardized achievement tests in mathematics, algebra and geometry. The Japanese have evolved a motivated, self-disciplined and efficient workforce which works hard for long hours and which saves a very high proportion of its income. They have developed a not-so-highly paid management committed to long-run corporate productivity and output growth, not to short-run profits or temporary advantage. They have achieved this with a very high rate of investment in plant and equipment.

The behaviour patterns of Japanese industrial growth are based on a long social history and cannot easily be transported to other parts of the world. However, the amazing economic growth of the other Asian rim economies – South Korea, Taiwan, Hong Kong and Singapore – which began slowly in the 1960s but accelerated rapidly by the late 1970s, suggests the workings of a broad Asian economic community.

The Japanese have highly efficient industries in steel and automobiles, advanced non-electrical machinery and machine tools. In addition they are now leaders in consumer electronics. These widely recognized successes are the principal bases of their penetration of the American market. But they are also making rapid progress in more advanced technology areas: new drugs and many industrial chemicals; fibre optics, a technology cluster that can serve as the basis for a huge market in telecommunications; robotics and machine tool technology; and high performance ceramics. They are emerging in several important areas of semiconductor technology including low-cost random memory access chips, high-density computer memories, and materials required to produce state-of-the-art computer chips. In important subsectors of computer hardware they now compete with American producers. They are potential competitors in aircraft technology. In summary, Japan threatens American supremacy in advanced technology.

Given these achievements, the Japanese are serious economic competitors. The possibility that they will take the lead in new products and processes based on advanced technologies raises threats to future job growth in the US and to American power and influence abroad. When added to the current job concerns of organized American labour in the more traditional areas of apparel, textiles, footwear, steel, construction and industrial machinery and automobiles, there is strong reason for the US to be concerned about Japanese competition.

'REINDUSTRIALIZATION' AND THE END OF THE TRADE DEFICIT

Dollar Depreciation

In the four-year period 1982–86, domestic demand for consumer goods, investment goods and government purchases grew at a rate of 5.1 per cent per year. Domestic output grew at the rate of 3.8 per cent per year. The difference was made up by goods imported from abroad. If the trade deficit is to be eliminated eventually, domestic production will have to grow faster than domestic spending, the difference representing goods shipped abroad. This, of course, will lower the growth of consumption and investment.

To balance the trade deficit, resources must be reallocated from their current use to the production of export goods and import-competing goods. This is mainly a problem for the manufacturing, mining and agricultural sectors of the economy. There are limits to the potential for increasing service exports. Contrary to popular myth, the United States is not becoming a service economy, at least as indexed by either the composition of domestic output or the proportion of exports that are services.

In the US as well as in other industrialized economies, the output of goods as opposed to services is a constant percentage of GNP over time. Employment, not output, in goods production has fallen relative to the service sector. The more rapid productivity advances in the goods-producing sectors than in the service sectors, has caused this decline.

Furthermore, it is primarily manufactured goods, raw materials and agricultural commodities that are exportable, not services. Aside from tourism, transportation and financial services, the possibility of exporting services is limited. They constitute only about 20 per cent of American exports of goods and services. Therefore, an increase in exported goods will require a major shift of resources from the service sector to the goods-producing sector, either by labour resources actually moving between sectors, or by new entrants to the labour force and new investment entering the goods-producing sector, or by activating idle and unemployed labour.

To eliminate the trade deficit and achieve the necessary reallocation of resources, requires about a 4 per cent shift in US productive capacity. This means that about four million workers would have to move to work in the foreign trade sector. In addition, there would have to be an expansion in plant capacity both in the form of buildings and equipment. This process of 'reindustrialization' requires difficult, but manageable, internal adjustments. Among other things, since idle resources are not available for this reallocation, it will mean considerable reduction in the growth of domestic consumption and investment.

For dollar depreciation to set this reallocation process in motion requires that several conditions be satisfied.[6] First, the change in the exchange rate must be viewed as permanent, not an easy determination to make when the exchange rate is a speculative variable. Second, exchange rate changes must be 'passed through' to the prices of imports and exports which is not always done when market shares (i.e., pricing to market) rather than profits (i.e., pricing to costs) are important to sellers. Third, import-competing industries must not raise prices under the umbrella of depreciation. Finally, importers must be sensitive to relative prices which is not the case when domestic output is a poor substitute for imports. With all of these 'slippages', the market process can be slow and uncertain.

There are reasons why the market process is sluggish. While the dollar has fallen against the yen and mark, it has not yet fallen significantly against the currencies of Latin America, the oil exporters, and the Newly Industrializing Countries of East Asia. Trade barriers might also have played some minor role in preventing adjustments. More importantly, however, it is because American goods are often very poor substitutes for foreign goods either because of quality or because the US simply does not make what it is importing. This fact has been partly masked by the behaviour of many foreign exporters who penetrated the American market with low dollar prices when the dollar appreciated, but who maintained their American market shares by not raising dollar import prices when the dollar depreciated.

The price of dollar imports, measured relative to domestically produced goods, fell by about 25 per cent during the same period in which the dollar appreciated by about 40 per cent. By the autumn of 1987 the dollar had fallen below its pre-appreciation level, yet the price of imports, relative to the price of import-competing goods, rose by less than 5 per cent. In light of this situation, it should not be surprising that dollar depreciation has been accompanied by rapidly increasing physical quantities of imports. The hope that dollar depreciation would discourage imports is being dashed by this pass-through problem. Of course, at some point dollar depreciation will force foreign exporters to raise their dollar prices, but then, low price elasticities might prevent significant adjustment in the quantity of imports.

On the other hand, the relative prices of American exports as seen by foreign buyers have been synchronized with the movement of the dollar. They rose by over 25 per cent during the period of dollar appreciation, 1981–85, and then fell back below – indeed, well below – their pre-appreciation level after the dollar began to fall in 1985. None the less, despite some growth in world income, the physical quantity of exports in the third quarter of 1987 was no more than 10 per cent above its level in 1980! This is to be compared to the physical quantity of imports which by the third quarter of 1987 were almost 60 per cent higher than their 1980 level. The response of exports relative to export price changes is quite muted, suggesting that US goods are not very good substitutes for those of their competitors.

Whenever the price system fails there is a search for solutions based on authority, not markets. This is the issue that has re-emerged in Western Europe in the debate over real wage adjustments versus Keynesian expansion. It was the issue in the United States in the 1970s when high energy prices pitted advocates of rationing and government research on alternative energy sources against proponents of market processes. It was the basic issue in the 1930s over how to re-employ the unemployed. And, it is now the issue with regard to the American trade deficit.

Protectionism

It has been over two years since the dollar began to depreciate and the trade deficit has not improved. An alternative is being considered – protectionism. It is not Smoot–Hawley, but it is protectionist. If America's trading partners who are in large surplus do not agree to take more American goods or refuse to institute orderly marketing arrangements, quotas or other restrictive measures will be used against them.

There are rumblings in this direction from the US Congress where blanket restrictions are being eschewed in favour of more aggressive negotiation on a bilateral commodity-by-commodity basis. This scheme may risk a trade war among trading nations, as happened in the 1930s. The result then was a decline in world trade, not an improvement in the US trade balance. Trade is a two-way street and for every deficit country there are one or more surplus countries. For the deficit country to restrict imports and successfully improve its trade balance implies that the surplus countries accept a reduction in their trade balances. Under the circumstance of forced unemployment, retaliation is likely.

However, there are forces that limit the possibility of intensified trade restrictions at this time. American export industries oppose them. The large and politically influential financial sector opposes any action which threatens the free world-wide movement of financial capital. The multinational corporations oppose restrictions on trade. The administration opposes them. Finally, the unemployment rate has fallen below 6 per cent, and this has weakened popular support for such action. Of course, none of these forces could withstand the spread of irrational and passionate decision-making caused by a sudden financial or political crisis.

Given the internal political problems in the various nations involved, it has proved difficult to reach a negotiated settlement on trade issues. Indeed, because there are so few bases of agreement, the frequent economic summits have deteriorated into publicity sessions, and the GATT meetings which seek multilateral agreements on trade reduction have not produced encouraging results. More likely than not, the world will limp along with increasing numbers of bilateral agreements, as nations wait and hope that the subtle workings of the market exchange rates – or something else – will do their magic.

Meanwhile, it should be kept in mind that much world trade is already subject to restrictions of one kind or another. The markets for agricultural products are protected and subsidized in Western Europe, Japan and the United States. Oil has been loosely cartelized. The newly-industrializing countries in East Asia and Latin America protect their infant industries with tariffs and quotas. Japan's inter-firm purchase relationships make it a difficult market to enter even though its tariffs are low. Western Europe has restrictive tariffs and quotas on many manufactured goods.

Even the US, which is the most open of all markets, has orderly marketing arrangements and quotas governing trade in steel, autos, footwear, apparel, textiles, military hardware and sugar. The export of potentially important military technology is restricted.

The world trading system has survived much interference and, except in a financial and production crisis, the international economy is not likely to balkanize under the current strain of unbalanced trade and unemployment.

A US Recession or a Western European and Japanese Expansion?
If exchange depreciation does not work and protection is either ineffective or politically unfeasible, then the US is left with the option of reducing financial ability to import. Lower real wages or higher unemployment will restrain imports, and these changes will take place if there is either an endogenous economic downturn or an adjustment in macroeconomic policies which initiate such a downturn.

The US economy has been expanding for over five years and it remains uncertain just when a downturn will occur. By raising taxes and reducing spending, the US might be able to restrain the financial ability of Americans to import. If the changes were large enough and consumers and businesses did not respond by simply reducing their savings, this could be an effective policy. Obviously, it would not be a popular policy, for it requires unemployment to reduce purchasing power.

While Congress and the administration believe that the budget deficit is too large, there are no signs of an emerging political coalition capable of embarking on a policy of budget restraint. While small changes in taxes or the defence budget might be introduced, they are irrelevant to the trade problem.

Even if the Japanese and Western Europeans were receptive to a negotiated settlement of macroeconomic policy differences between them and the United States, successful negotiation is unlikely to occur unless the US were able to achieve greater control of its budget process. Meanwhile, the Western Europeans are caught in a political dilemma of their own. Conservatives do not want to increase budget deficits, due to fear of inflation and a further increase in interest obligations and the size of governments.

As in the 1920s, the claim is lodged that Western European unemployment is due to excessively high real wages, not insufficient aggregate demand. It is contended that demand expansion will not work. Unfortunately, this old controversy cannot be settled empirically. Politically the conservatives remain in power and resist American demands for them to expand. It would appear that the US must proceed on its own.

The American trade deficit has prompted some talk in the United States to seek Japanese assistance in the defence of the Pacific and oil. But without full-scale rearmament of Japan, which the US does not seek and the Japanese do not want, defence sharing will not significantly affect the American deficit *vis-à-vis* Japan. Instead, it is hoped that the Japanese would greatly expand internal consumption. Of particular interest is the idea that the Japanese can massively expand their housing stock, their purchase of manufactured consumer products, and their purchase of American agricultural products. It is highly unlikely, however, that the Japanese will imitate the American consumption patterns in housing, food or other goods. As with Western Europe, if the Japanese choose not to expand their economy, the US must proceed in isolation.

THE AMERICAN STANDARD OF LIVING

A reduction in the US trade deficit achieved through dollar depreciation or trade restraint, will lower the standard of living for the average American family as more goods are exported and less are imported. This decline in living standards would be even more intense if domestic recession corrected the trade deficit.

This will add downward pressure on real compensation per hour worked by wage and salary workers, which has been stagnating since 1973. At no time in the twentieth century has there been such a long period of stagnant real wages. Interestingly, families have been partially successful at sustaining the rate of growth in their consumption per person even in the face of stagnant real wages. Wives have gone to work. Young married couples have delayed or forgone having children. Savings rates have fallen. Families have borrowed. Yet despite these efforts, the growth in real consumption per capita has been decelerating since the early 1970s. This rate was 2.6 per cent per year in the 1960s, 2.3 per cent in the 1970s and 1.7 per cent in the 1980s.

For the first time since the Great Depression, the young do not anticipate doing as well as their parents. In America, a nation dedicated to rising living standards, the implications of this changing vision of the future are profound. America is a polyglot nation where not only equality of opportunity but growing opportunity are essential for long-run social and political stability. The stagnation of real wages thwarts this stabilizing process.

The wage slowdown results from a combination of forces, the most important being the slowdown in productivity growth since 1973. Since increased female participation rates, low savings rates, low birth rates and high imports cannot be sustained indefinitely, per capita consumption growth cannot be sustained. Only improved productivity can rescue this situation.

The rise in manufacturing productivity in the past three years is a promising sign in this regard. However, productivity in the service sector continues to stagnate and the manufacturing advance might not be sustainable. There remains a real threat to the continuation of the high American living standards.

CONCLUSIONS

America is faced with a collection of economic problems. It has large trade and budget deficits. Its real wages are stagnant. Its productivity is growing slowly. Its internal political process is in disarray. It cannot reach agreement with its allies on how to solve the Third World debt controversy, how to balance trade, or how to regulate international finance. The absence of domestic and international political agreement has driven the United States to an internal economic policy of *laissez-faire* and it has driven the world economy to the international counterpart. The result has been mixed.

The long American expansion has provided the world economy with markets, and has delayed or perhaps even prevented world-wide depression. However, during the past five years the world economy has been battered by speculation, massive trade imbalances, destablilizing financial capital flows and excessive unemployment. Without the ability to reach domestic and international political agreements on stable exchange rates, coordinated domestic macroeconomic policies and related political settlements, there remains a threat of world depression.

An elimination of the American trade deficit and a reduction in the budget deficit are alleged to be significant adjustments that will help stabilize the world economy. No matter how desirable these deficit reductions might seem towards reducing burdens on future American generations, budget balancing would not necessarily have a stabilizing effect on the world economy.

If accompanied by a weakening private economy, an effort to reduce the budget deficit by means of a significant tax increase will only intensify recessionary forces. While declining purchasing power would certainly discourage imports, American consumption and investment would fall as well. The American economy and the world economy would suffer a deflationary blow.

If managed recession is technically or politically impossible, the trade balance will require either a further fall in the dollar, additional trade restraints, or a German and Japanese economic expansion. Unfortunately, these measures are either slow in their effect or politically unacceptable. Thus the trade deficit will probably continue, being moderated by depreciation, but not being significantly affected until a market-determined and prolonged recession substantially reduces it.

While the trade deficit will eventually improve with continued depreciation of the dollar, market adjustment is tediously slow. Furthermore, it is not at all likely to correct more than a small portion of the deficit problem. But with collective action politically impossible, reliance on this market process is perhaps the only real option available. The market, with all its imperfections, becomes the only option available in a politically fragmented system. Managed recession, international macroeconomic coordination, trade restrictions, and political agreements on the Third World debt problem are all unlikely at this time.

In many respects the budget deficit is less of a problem than the trade deficit. Of course, most economists and politicians who castigate budget deficits because they encourage profligate consumption and excessive imports, are not consciously promoting recession. Rather we may rationalize their thinking by assuming that what they propose to eliminate is secular or continuous deficits and then only when full employment prevails. Under these conditions, they think that a reduction in the budget deficit will permanently increase the proportion of income that is invested and hope that it will reduce the structural trade deficit as well.

A tax increase would in the long run probably increase the proportion of income that is invested. It would also force a decline in government spending which is politically more palatable when it is financed by selling bonds rather than raising taxes. However, despite the positive secular relationship between budget and trade deficits in the past fifteen years, there is no mechanism other than recession for tax increases reliably and permanently to reduce imports. The structural component of the American trade deficit is a problem in technology and product quality.

Improving productivity in the production of existing products will not really take very far the task of improving the trade situation. Nor will cutting the real wage rate. After all, a 40 per cent depreciation has not been visibly effective and it takes a long time in annual productivity improvement to achieve the pricing equivalent of such large depreciations.

New and better tradeable products are required to eliminate the structural component of the American trade deficit. Balanced growth and exchange rate adjustments will be inadequate. In part, the process of improving the long-run competitive position of American producers requires that the average worker and manager pay closer attention to detail, and this is sometimes achieved when the educational and training process is improved. However, given the weakness of the American family structure and the high divorce rate, given the high level of alcoholism and drug abuse, given the high teenage pregnancy rate, given the disintegration of many of the American communities, and given the poor motivation of many people, an improvement in the self-discipline and self-confidence of the American workforce will be difficult to achieve by simply spending more money on the schools.

But if workers and managers cannot be properly motivated, then we must improve the quality and diversity of our products by improving our hard technology. This will require more scientists and engineers and more private and public spending on R & D. Tax incentives could help to stimulate R & D. Direct government support for commercial R & D by means of a new national agency could help, but the prospects for this are not promising. Industry would probably not agree on how to allocate funds, while the public would view these subsidies as unacceptable.

In recent years it has proved difficult to co-mingle military and commercial R & D. Earlier, there was substantial spillover from the military to the commercial sector, especially in the computer and aerospace sectors. There is some evidence that the spillovers now might be smaller. None the less, it is very probable that only through the military is a large, public R & D effort possible. Disconcerting though this conclusion might be, it appears that in the current American political environment, only militarily supported, commercial R & D programmes can cut their way through the political morass.

Any serious and successful attempt to reduce the American trade and budget deficits will mean a decline in the level of American consumption. This is the true meaning of deficit reduction. After a long period of weak productivity growth, the United States faces the prospect of austerity. This problem has been masked by the huge trade deficit and to a lesser extent by the budget deficit, but it cannot be masked forever.

NOTES

1. The problem with debt is not unique to the government sector. A rising ratio of corporate debt relative to equity or of consumer debt relative to consumer net worth could manufacture a debt crisis if a recession were to occur and both corporations and consumers were unable to repay obligated interest. Indeed, Kaufman and others quite rightly claim that the explosion in debt financing has made the economy increasingly vulnerable to a downturn in economic activity.
2. The argument that since 1973 the exchange rate has been a speculative variable rooted in varying expectations, driven by shocks, overshooting and speculative bubbles is developed carefully in the work of one of my students, Lawrence Krause.
3. Keynes, of course, stressed the psychological component in the interest rate determination process. John Garrett, a former student of mine, has argued quite persuasively that in the period 1918–32 the Fed, along with the major Central Banks of Western Europe, and under the leadership of Chairman Strong, struggled to gain control over market expectations, a precondition for controlling the creation of credit and the interest rate.
4. This argument is developed fully in Rapping (1984), Rapping and Bennett (1983), and Pulley and Rapping (1985) which appear elsewhere in this volume. It is not often that the weakness of the Fed. is mentioned in the public press but recently, Leonard Silk stressed the point in the New York Times, April 15, 1988
5. For an interesting perspective on Reaganomics, the reader is referred to Tobin's discussion of the subject in his collected policy essays.
6. For a rather extensive treatment of the issues raised in this section, the reader should consult the work of Petri and Gerlach.

REFERENCES

Bailey, Martin Neil. 'An Analysis of the Productivity Growth Decline' Unpublished paper prepared for the Panel on Technology and Employment, National Academy of Sciences, 1986.

Barro, Robert J. 'Are Government Bonds Net Worth?' *Journal of Political Economy*, **82**, November – December, 1972, 1095–117.

Committee on Science, Engineering and Public Policy, *Balancing the National Interest: U.S. National Security Export Controls and Global Economic Competition* (Washington, DC: National Academy Press, 1987).

Costrell, Robert M. 'The Impact of Technical Progress on Productivity, Wages and the Distribution of Employment'. In David Mowry and Richard M. Cyert (eds)

Studies in Technological Change, Employment and Policy (Cambridge, Mass: Ballinger, 1988).

Cyert Richard M. 'The Plight of Manufacturing,' *Issues in Science and Technology*, 1, 87–100.

Flamm, Kenneth. *Targeting the Computer* (Washington, DC: Brookings Institution, 1987).

——, 'The Changing Pattern of Industrial Robot Use'. In David Mowry and Richard M. Cyert (eds) *Studies in Technological Change. Employment and Policy* (Cambridge Mass: Ballinger, 1988).

Garrett, John R. *The Postwar International Financial Order, 1918–1932* (Unpublished Ph.D. Dissertation, University of Massachusetts, 1985).

Gibney, Frank. *Japan: The Fragile Superpower* (New York: Meridian Books, 1985).

Griliches, Zvi. *R & D, Patents and Productivity* (Chicago: University of Chicago Press, 1984).

Hakkio, Craig S. and Roberts, Richard. 'Has the Dollar Fallen Far Enough', *Economic Review*, Federal Reserve Bank of Kansas City, July/August, 1987.

Kaufman, Henry. *Interest Rates, the Markets and the New Financial World* (New York: Times Books, 1986).

Krause, Lawrence A. *A Theoretical and Empirical Examination of Speculation in the Foreign Exchange Market: A Search for Speculative Bubbles* (Unpublished Ph.D. Dissertation, University of Massachusetts, 1988).

Leontief, Wassily and Duchin, Fay. *The Future Impact of Automation on Workers* (New York: Oxford University Press, 1986).

Lerner, Abba P. *The Economics of Control* (London: Macmillan, 1944).

Lucas, Robert E. *Studies in Business Cycle Theory* (Cambridge, Mass: MIT Press, 1981).

National Research Council, *Measurement and Interpretation of Productivity*. Panel to Review Productivity Statistics, Albert Rees, Chairman (Washington, DC: National Academy Press, 1979).

National Science Board, *Science Indicators, 1985 Report* (Washington, DC: U.S. Government Printing Office, 1986).

Petri, Peter and Gerlach, Stefan. (eds) *Economics of the Dollar Cycle* (Cambridge, Mass: MIT Press, forthcoming).

Podgursky, Michael. 'Job Displacement and Labor Market Adjustment: Evidence from the Displaced Worker Survey'. In David Mowry and Richard M. Cyert (eds). *Studies in Technological Change, Employment and Policy* (Cambridge, Mass : Ballinger, 1988).

Sargent, Thomas J. *Rational Expectations and Inflation* (New York: Harper and Row, 1986).

Simon, Herbert A. *Reason in Human Affairs* (Stanford, Ca.: Stanford University Press, 1983).

Solow, Robert M. and Blinder, Alan. 'Analytical Foundations of Fiscal Policy'. In *The Economics of Public Finance* (Washington, DC: Brookings Institution, 1974).

Tobin, James. *Policies for Prosperity: Essays in the Keynesian Mode* (Cambridge, Mass : MIT Press, 1987).

2 Real Wages, Productivity and Technology*

INTRODUCTION

The ability of the United States to regain its role as the dominant military and political power in the Western Alliance, as the leading financial centre of the global economy, and as a leading world industrial power, requires that it be able to reignite a sustained rate of technological innovation, technological diffusion and overall advancing productivity. A weakening of technological advance and productivity growth, or a permanent slowdown of the United States relative to other countries, will undermine American leadership. In turn, advancing productivity requires a high rate of domestic investment coupled with developments in both 'hard technology', as embodied in machines, and 'soft technology', as embodied in dedicated and self-disciplined managers and workers coupled with effective workplace organization.

Sustained, rapid growth in productivity and technology permit the nation to compete effectively in world markets by reducing the costs of existing products and by introducing new products and techniques. New products and processes, coupled with steep learning curves, permit the maintenance of monopoly rents and balance of trade advantages. At the same time, advancing productivity means a rising domestic standard of living. In democratic, industrial societies, improvements in living standards are essential for morale and social stability. Without advances in productivity and technology, long-run competitiveness can only be

*Written in the summer of 1987.

maintained by a continuously depreciating currency with an associated downward pressure on domestic living standards. This threatens the nation's willingness and ability to continue its role as a world leader.

THE SLOWDOWN IN PRODUCTIVITY AND REAL WAGE GROWTH

Starting in 1973 the growth rate of productivity began to slow down (see Table 2.1). It is easier to measure than explain this productivity slowdown. In the most general sense, the productivity slowdown is attributable to either poor motivation and inadequate skill on the part of workers and managers, or to the inability to increase and improve the quantity and quality of the capital stock, that is, the tools and machines with which people work.

Of the many problems confronting the American economy, perhaps the most important is this disappointing performance of labour productivity – defined as output per hour worked – and of multifactor productivity – defined as output per combined unit of capital, labour and raw materials – during the 1970s and 1980s. Between 1948 and 1973, labour productivity in the entire economy grew at the rate of about 2.5 per cent per year. Then disaster struck. From 1973 to 1985, labour productivity grew at the rate of only about 0.6 of one per cent per year. The slowdown was world-wide.

It is this poor productivity experience that in part – indeed in large part – explains the failure of average real wages to advance significantly in the period after the 1973 oil price shock (see Table 2.1). Between 1948 and 1973, real wages per hour worked (including fringe benefits) grew at the rate of 2.7 per cent per annum. At this annual growth rate, the income of the average worker would double every 23 years. In this age of abundance, Americans were optimistic. Their living standards were higher than those of their parents. Their children's living standards would be higher than their own. In America, where men and women judge their intrinsic worth by their ability to make money and consume, it seemed to all that the nation had fulfilled its destiny. It had delivered its children to the Promised Land.

However, the growth rate in earnings in the first 25 years after World War II dwarfs the subsequent rate of growth. Between 1973 and 1985, real compensation per hour worked grew at the modest rate of only 0.2 of 1 per cent a year. At this rate, it would take 347 years for wages to double. Americans struggled to maintain

Table 2.1 Percentage change per Year in aggregate labour productivity and average hourly real compensation, selected periods, 1948–85

	1948–85	1948–57	1957–66	1966–73	1973–79	1979–85
Labour productivity growth rate[a]	1.9	2.5	3.0	1.9	0.45	0.85
Real compensation per hour, growth rate[b]	1.9	3.4	2.5	2.1	0.36	−0.18

Sources: Robert M. Costrell, 'The Impact of Technical Progress on Productivity, Wages, and the Distribution of Employment: Theory and Post War Experience in the U.S.', A Report to the National Academy of Sciences, Panel on Technology and Employment, August 1987.
a. Productivity is measured as GNP per hour worked. For the entire period 1948-85, Costrell concludes that capital deepening accounts for only two-fifths of the productivity advance while total factor productivity accounts for three-fifths.
b. Average compensation per hour covers all wage and salary workers and includes fringe benefits. These data on real compensation are sensitive to the choice of deflator, but the general pattern of changes in the post-war period are unaffected by this choice.

previous consumption standards. They borrowed from abroad. They worked longer hours and more members of the family went to work. They had fewer children and the birth rate fell to an historic low. The result was a profound impact on the social structure and on the nature of the family. Americans were being pushed from the Promised Land back into an economic and social wilderness.

MOTIVATION, ORGANIZATION AND TECHNOLOGY

Those who claim that poor motivation, inadequate self-discipline, weak ambition and poor skills are the causes of the productivity problem, search for some policy that will modify behaviour. With this emphasis, one is quickly led to a reappraisal of training and education in the schools, homes and workplaces. Those who stress this individual or the human capital component have also been rethinking the way in which the workplace is organized, with particular attention to incentives. In the 1980s a variety of experiments at reorganizing industrial relations have been introduced by American industry, especially in unorganized plants and offices. Statistical evidence on these efforts is unavailable although they probably have been modestly beneficial.

On the other hand, for those who stress the failure of technology –limited innovation and slow diffusion of new methods and new products – it is necessary to search for some means of increasing the rate of new discovery and its commerical introduction. This leads inevitably to consideration of the financing and organization of research and development, the incentive system under which managers evaluate the risks of introducing new technology, the extent to which workers and communities can adapt to change, and the overall level of investment in new plant and equipment.

There is no general agreement on how much of the productivity problem can be attributed to worker and managerial performance problems and how much to the failure of technology. There is a presumption that in the production of goods, where tasks are structured, technology is relatively most important, while in non-goods production, individual initiative, attentiveness, and motivation play a more significant role. Unfortunately, neither the concept of motivation nor the concept of technology can easily be measured. As Solow pointed out in his famous 1957 article, all that we can observe is the interactive result of these two forces as reflected in some measure of productivity such as output per person-hour.

Sometimes an effort will be made to identify motivation through indirect measures such as absenteeism rates, number of grievances filed, or error rates in some production processes. And sometimes skill and motivation are indexed by years of school completed or years of on-the-job experience. In the same vein technological change may be indexed by the number of patents granted, by the number of engineers employed, or by the amount of money spent on research and development.

As imperfect as these measures are, we have very little else to go on other than the sometimes questionable reliability of expert opinion, which is occasionally influenced by financial or professional interest in the outcome of their judgements. Science and research are big business in the United States. The outcome of the scientific and engineering research process is highly uncertain and this sometimes permits proponents of particular projects to make outlandish claims based on their personal or institutional authority, not the inherent merit of the projects.

To make matters more complex, our understanding of production processes is really quite limited. The economist studies these problems at a fairly general level of aggregation, relating broadly measured inputs to changes in broadly measured outputs. Changes in output not attributable to measured inputs are called 'technical change'. This concept of technical change can range from the introduction of a steam engine, to the introduction of a computer for inventory control, to increased worker motivation, to a newly built highway connecting two points, to quality control circles or social innovations such as a customs union.

THE MICROECONOMIC EVIDENCE ON TECHNOLOGY, MOTIVATION AND SKILL

In an attempt to find subsidiary evidence on what might constitute technical change, there have been several 'case studies' on such matters as the profitability of productivity enhancement. There have been a wide range of studies on the private and social rate of return on specific machine-embodied or product-embodied innovations, and on the relationship between R & D and productivity growth. Studies since the late 1950s by Griliches, Mansfield, Minasian, and other academic as well as business researchers have found both very high productivity effects from R & D and very high rates of return from specific innovations. The estimated rates of return are often as high as 50 or 60 per cent per year. These and related studies contain a strong presumption that technological not social innovations are the quantitatively most important part of what is called in the aggregate, 'technical change'. These studies do not deny, however, that there may be certain organizational and motivational preconditions for the successful introduction of new technology.

The organization of the workplace with fixed machines and methods determines static productivity. The process of introducing new machines and methods is continuous. The success of this dynamic process depends on the adaptability of individuals and hierarchical social systems in the workplace. As people adapt to the requirements of new methods, they must adjust their behaviour patterns, learn new social relations and aquire new skills. When it is working properly, training and education is at the core of a system of instruction designed to enable people to adapt to their changing environment.

A set of studies similar to the studies mentioned above have also been done on what is called 'human capital', that complex mix of skill, attitude and motivation that determines an individual's productivity. Studies by Mincer, Becker and their students have provided a rather large body of evidence on the rates of return to formal education, experience and on-the-job training. These studies generally suggest high but falling rates of return on training and education in the post-war years. In related efforts, researchers have found very high returns to literacy in many underdeveloped economies. These findings along with much indirect evidence on the value of human capital – e.g. the post-war recoveries of Germany and Japan despite the complete destruction of their physical capital and the highly productive labour forces of East Asia where motivation and self-discipline seem important – suggest that the human capital contribution to productivity might be very large.

SOME DIFFICULTIES IN IDENTIFYING THE PRODUCTIVITY IMPACT OF TECHNOLOGY

An innovation is the commercial application of an existing invention or idea. There is often a very long time-lag from invention or discovery to the time of its commercial introduction. Automatic drive was invented in 1904, but was not commercially introduced until 1939, a lag of thirty-five years. Penicillin was accidentally discovered by Flemming in 1922 but not used as a drug until 1941, a lag of nineteen years. The jet engine was invented in 1928 but not applied until 1941 when the Germans used it on military aircraft. This was a lag of thirteen years. The transistor, an electrical on-off 'switch', was invented in 1940 and first applied ten years later.

Aside from the lag between discovery and innovation, the spread of new technology across firms and households is often a very slow process depending on the uncertainty of financial payoffs. As profitability increases the speed of introduction also increases. As uncertainty decreases, the speed of introduction also increases. Some studies suggest that an industry might take from 10 to 15 years from the initial application of a new technology to its widespread use. A technology does not spread very rapidly across industry when it is only marginally profitable or when there is uncertainty about its cost and productivity.

Some economists have a Schumpeterian view that innovations in both processes and products are bunched rather than distributed randomly over time. When there are many potential innovations available and when investment expands to introduce these innovations, economic activity also expands, resulting in prosperity. When there are few potential innovations, there is no basis for increased investment and output stagnates. Innovations – introduced by engineers and entrepreneurs – are based on prior discoveries made by scientists and engineers. It is, therefore, the scientists, engineers and entrepreneurs who according to the Schumpeterian view drive the economy.

This view is popular among engineers and many business leaders in the United States who believe in a scientific and technological solution to declining U.S. international competitiveness. This view is also popular in Europe where high unemployment rates have given rise to the argument that there is need for a technological basis for renewed economic growth. It is argued that clusters of technology based on microelectronics, biotechnology and materials technology will underpin this new era of growth.

Emphasizing economic, not technical, efficiency, economists are not intellectually predisposed to the idea of revolutionary technical change. Instead they think in terms of the slow and steady process of innovation and diffusion. For them it is the interaction of tens of thousands of minor modifications and patents, each developed around broad technology clusters, that slowly work their way through the economy. Like 'Old Man River', technology just keeps rolling along: there are no revolutionary technologies and technologies do not bunch in certain periods. Except for the accelerating effect of aggregate demand or chance, technological change remains even over time. Economists suspect that computer technology and other technologies like advanced materials or bio-technology might generate productivity advances, but the process will be slow and the outcome uncertain.

The Schumpeterian position must be distinguished from two other positions on Western European unemployment. The Keynesians who see the buyers of goods and services – consumers, businessmen and politicians – as moving the economy, argue that it is fiscal stringency which accounts for high unemployment. The monetarists, on the other hand, whose important players are the bankers and financiers, argue that real wage inflexibility is the problem. A similar set of issues is raised in the United States where the monetarists attribute the rapid employment growth of the past decade to real wage flexibility and the Keynesians attribute the employment expansion to large budget deficits.

Let us consider the view that technology is revolutionary, not evolutionary, somewhat further. Innovations improve as they spread across firms within an industry, and across industries. For example, the modern airplane is a far different machine from the plane first flown by the Wright brothers. The first integrated circuits crammed hundreds of on-off switches, or transistors, onto a silicon wafer. Later came the capability for thousands, then tens of thousands of switches. More and more memory and computer capacity was packed into smaller and smaller containers. The number of innovation improvements that occur in any given year cannot be counted because of the difficulty in defining what we mean by an improvement. Yet it is clear that every technology cluster – the computer, the airplane, plastics – undergoes thousands of day-to-day changes instituted by workers, foremen and research engineers. This process is neatly documented by Gilfillan in describing the technology of water transportation from the floating log to the modern military naval vessel.

Nor can we measure what one might call generic innovations unless we are willing to accept that judgement of experts who use a common language to list the major innovations of a particular era. In the recent period this list would include such things as the jet engine, the transistor and the rocket. Experts might be able to agree on such a list but there are no objective units which permit us to count and then weight basic innovations by their importance in terms of production efficiency or their contribution to the growth of new consumer product markets. Newly-designed aircraft engines may be less important than, say, the transistor, but by how much? We are left with the rather unfortunate conclusion that technology cannot be measured easily except by certain social or political conventions in the use of language.

Data on the number of patents do not permit us to solve this problem, since they do not distinguish between the patent that will greatly impact on productivity and the patent that will never be commericalized. What is needed is a way of distinguishing the potential effect of the patented idea on productivity.

Without an obvious way to measure innovations we are unable to count the number of innovations occurring in different time-periods or in different industries. We therefore cannot accurately or even crudely test the question of whether periods of economic expansion are a result of new process and product technologies, as opposed to the more common view that the business cycle is a demand-led process and ultimately a monetary phenomenon. Despite obvious limitations, the monetary stock, the quantity of credit, and the government deficit are easier to measure than technological innovations.

An indirect measure of technology is based on the notion that any increase in the productivity of both capital and labour, what is called total factor productivity, must indirectly index an improvement in technology. However, as previously mentioned, total factor productivity overstates the amount of 'technical change' that is occurring. It confounds changes in the behaviour of labour and management with improvements in machines and new methods. While we cannot easily separate improvements in the effectiveness of labour or management from improvements embodied in our machines, certain informal judgements are possible, based on reason, common experience, and bits and pieces of subsidiary, formal evidence.

EXPLAINING THE PRODUCTIVITY SLOWDOWN OF THE 1970s

The productivity of labour depends on experience, training and motivation. The 1970s witnessed a large increase in the number of new workers because of the baby-boom generation (1947–61) entering the labour market and because of the increased labour force participation of inexperienced women. From 1957 to 1979 the proportion of adult males among employed workers fell from 55 per cent to 44 per cent. These developments probably reduced the average experience level of the labour force and thus might have reduced aggregate productivity. On the other hand, there was a continuing increase in the average education level of the new labour force entrants as measured by years of school completed. These two tendencies were probably offsetting. The compositional changes in the labour force therefore would not explain the decline in productivity.

It is widely believed that starting in the mid- or late 1960s there was a deterioration in the average quality of education as measured by numerical reasoning, written and oral communication, problem-solving and literacy. Causal empiricism by American educators, as well as SAT scores and other test data support this view.

The causes of this development were many. The decline in the size of the school-age population turned education into a declining industry with an ageing workforce. Low teacher morale and lack of enthusiasm and inventiveness resulted in blocked opportunities for young and talented teachers. The system suffered from general bureaucratic sclerosis. Meanwhile, there was a reaction against traditional authority and meritocracy by the egalitarian social movements of the late 1960s which undermined the learning process. Additionally, increasing affluence and suburbanization in the post-war years led a younger generation to lose sight of the hard work and sacrifices of the previous generation which had produced this affluence.

These factors should not be overlooked in a full explanation of the decline in aggregate productivity. However, except perhaps in the service sector, they are not likely to account for more than a small part of the slowdown. In industries like construction, mining and durable goods manufacturing, where the proportion of young and women workers is small, and where the workers have transited the school system before the decline in cognitive performance and before the change in social attitudes, the productivity slowdown was quite in evidence over the period 1973–79.

The non-goods-producing sector, sometimes referred to as the 'service' sector, consists of such activities as health care, retailing, sales of financial and real assets, and preparation and serving of food. In all industrial economies, this sector has over this entire century grown relative to the goods-producing sector. In the US, some 50 per cent of employed workers were in the goods-producing sector in the 1920s. Now, only 25 per cent of the employed workers produce goods. Apparently, growth in productivity is greater in the production of goods than in the production of services, although this assertion should be viewed with some caution since there are difficulties in measuring most service outputs. However, the process of shifting employment from the goods to the service sector did not sufficiently accelerate in the early 1970s to provide a promising explanation for the slowdown in productivity.

The productivity slowdown was not due to the sluggishness in capital formation, which seemed to proceed at the normal rate when measured relative to GNP. However, the labour force was growing at an accelerating rate after 1973. With capital formation proceeding at only its normal rate, new workers may not have been supplied with an adequate quantity of machines and tools with which to work. While this reduction in the capital – labour ratio probably slowed productivity growth, various studies find that this effect can account for no more than one-quarter of the slowdown.

In goods production, of which manufacturing is the quantitatively most important, the most promising explanation of the slowdown is that the process of innovation – the commerical introduction of new techniques often embodied in machines – slowed. Supporters of this view often cite a sharp reduction in R & D spending starting in the late 1960s and a reduction in the flow of patents which also started in the late 1960s. They also cite the two oil price shocks and the shifting distribution of world production, with its concomitant uncertainty and requirement that business managers devote more time and energy to managing these changes, leaving less time to oversee new innovations unrelated to energy conservation. Moreover, managers began to concentrate on the present and the immediate future rather than engaging in strategic planning. New innovations often require the long view.

In the production of non-goods, the continued sluggishness of productivity at these unstructured tasks might also reflect, to a relatively large extent, a decline in motivation and attentiveness. Causal empiricism supports this allegation, but we should not lose sight of the fact that the outstanding performance of productivity in the non-goods sector in the 1950s and 1960s might be the anomaly, not the slowdown in the 1970s and 1980s.

THE INCREASE IN MANUFACTURING PRODUCTIVITY IN THE 1980s

As we turn to the current economic expansion we note that the productivity growth has increased. In particular, manufacturing productivity has dramatically improved although in the non-manufacturing sector – save for communications where productivity never really slowed down – the productivity slowdown continues. Because this sector is so large in terms of employment, the growth in manufacturing productivity is unable to significantly lift aggregate productivity. In the period 1973–79, aggregate productivity grew at the rate of only 0.45 per cent per year. This figure was higher in the 1979–85 period, 0.85 per cent per year, but still well below the pre-1973 level.

The recent improvement in manufacturing productivity is an important development. Those who argue that the productivity slowdown was a failure to introduce new technology would now argue that the improvement is the result of an increase in the number and diffusion of innovations. The increase in commercial and government (military and non-military) R & D starting in the late 1970s, the increase in the number of patents in the early 1980s, and the fall in oil prices lends some credence to this argument.

There is the possibility that the favourable productivity experience will be short-lived. Starting in the recession of the early 1980s and continuing under the pressure of foreign import competition, many manufacturing firms eliminated excess workers, both in offices and on plant floors. They closed many inefficient plants and in some cases replaced them with new facilities. This process of eliminating excess labour and capacity might have temporarily increased productivity in the manufacturing sector. I should add that it is sometimes argued that productivity was enhanced by the takeover movement in the US, but empirical evidence on this proposition is limited. I suspect that the argument is false.

Even if the improved rate of productivity growth in manufacturing were permanent, productivity has not increased outside manufacturing. With labour force growth now slowing and efforts being made to restrict immigration, a shortage of labour is likely to develop which will stimulate the search for labour substitutes in all industries including those in the service sector.

Perhaps this will stimulate productivity growth in the service sector. But if service sector productivity cannot be improved, we have then entered into a period of permanent stagnation of the real wage rate, and this might eventually be the fate of all advanced industrial societies.

MICROELECTRONICS TECHNOLOGY

There has been in recent years a rather optimistic view that microelectronic technology could serve as the basis for a large increase in productivity both in the office and the factory. The rapid fall in the cost of computing power – embedding the power of earlier computer bemoths in small desk-size computers – greatly reduces the cost of storing, retrieving and transmitting information. This technology cluster includes computers, telecommunication equipment and the electronic components on which these technologies are based.

In telecommunications, computer-based switching has replaced the mechanical switching process. This has greatly reduced equipment costs and because the new electronic-based process is so compact, the large real estate costs of the older, bulkier system have been eliminated. This industry has also introduced automatic billing systems, satellite transmission and other improved transmission processes which have reduced costs. Moreover, the computers have replaced many telephone operators and repair personnel. The computer-based cost savings in this industry have been large.

There have also been significant cost reductions in the banking industry where electronic tellers, on-line access to accounts, and computer-aided cheque processing have all reduced costs. Gains have also been made in other parts of the finance industry, where domestic and international markets have been tightly linked by rapid communications.

In manufacturing there are several important actual or potential uses of microelectronic technologies.[1] These include robotics, electronically controlled machine tools, computer-aided design, automated guided vehicles and computer-controlled reliability testing and expert systems. Many of these technologies have been separately introduced into the production process in 'isolated islands' of computer technologies.

Robots are used to weld and paint in auto plants where most industrial robots are found. Industrial robots are also used in the assembly of some electrical components. A more limited number of robots are found in industries which make precision machinery, metal-processing machinery and metal products. Less sophisticated robots are used in foundries and in the making of plastic components. In general, however, the total number of robots in use remains quite limited in the US and abroad, although both Japan and Sweden are ahead of the US in the manufacture and industrial use of robots. There is some hope that with the eventual development of better sensors (the capability to distinguish shapes and colour) or with the improved design of parts which would simplify the assembly process, the number of robots will increase significantly.

Throughout the manufacturing sector computers are increasingly used to aid in the design of parts. Computer-aided, numerically-controlled machine tools are used to fabricate parts by cutting, bending and shaping them. There are some automated assembly processes such as IBM's assembly plant for computer printers. There are many computer stations used for monitoring product quality. Yet all of these uses still represent a limited use of computers in manufacturing in comparison to the gigantic number of tasks that must be performed.

The long-run goal of microelectronic technology is to link the many islands of computer uses into an integrated process which is itself computer-controlled. In computer-aided manufacturing a series of machine tools which make parts, linked by a computer to automatically guided vehicles, in turn take these parts to a series of robots for assembly. If the design process were also automatically linked to the production and assembly process, we would have something called computer-aided design/computer-aided manu-facturing, or CAD/CAM. The next step in automation would link together the planning of materials use, the detailed sequence of manufacturing operations, sales databases, and accounting and financial procedures, all tied together into an integrated whole requiring limited human intervention. This long-run goal of Computer-Integrated Manufacturing is still in the idea stage both here and abroad.

The advance in manufacturing productivity in recent years cannot be attributed to the computer as an aid in design and assembly. Its use is still too limited. Even in the auto industry where computer use is concentrated, productivity change is only in small part a result of computers. However, there has been a significant increase in the number of computer-based work stations in the offices of America. Perhaps this can account for the growth in manufacturing productivity.

Almost 25 per cent of the investment in productive equipment in 1984 was in personal computers, copying machines and related office equipment. Some 60 per cent of office work stations are now computerized. There has also been a significant improvement in intra- and inter- office communications systems. Although office productivity measurement is difficult, it appears to date that the impact of computers on office productivity has been limited. However, these new systems are expected to have a significant effect on future office productivity. In 1984, there were 16.7 million clerical jobs, almost 16 per cent of the workforce. Therefore, if office computerization will eventually enhance office productivity, future productivity advances in clerical areas might significantly affect total productivity in both the goods and non-goods sectors of the economy.

THE POLICY ISSUES AND CONCLUSIONS

In the 1930s the basic problem in the United States was mass unemployment. Today, the basic problem is the stagnation of real wages. The only hope for correcting this situation is to improve productivity. There are several policy actions that are relevant to the problems of technology and productivity. These include efforts to improve both our primary and secondary school systems as well as stimulate interest in science and technology. They also include efforts to increase the rate of machine-embodied technical change including more investment and R & D, discouraging financial market speculation and encouraging managers to think in long-run terms, which would increase their interest in new technology and change.

Training and educational policy

Recent evidence indicates that American students have been performing poorly, both in comparison to earlier generations and in comparison to students in other countries, especially Japan. The poor average performance of American students at problem-solving, numerical reasoning and language skills is compounded by the fact that the functional illiteracy rate is high in the US, even among the young.

There is a national campaign led by the Carnegie Foundation, the Department of Education, corporate leaders, and educators to ignite interest in this problem. These efforts coupled with the seriousness of the problem itself, have led to some attempts at the local level to improve the situation. The federal government is not inclined to interfere, although aid to education is a political issue. With the federal budget in deficit, state governments which are now in surplus must generate the funds for school improvement. But, without stronger family units, cohesive neighbourhood systems, dedicated school administrators and teachers, and state governments committed to improvement, funds may not help.

There is also concern that the United States is not graduating enough engineers and that the best students are going into law, finance and business, not science and engineering. In 1983, the US graduated 73,000 engineering students with bachelors degrees, 19,000 with master degrees and 3,000 with Ph.Ds. When it is recognized that 56 per cent of the American Ph.Ds in 1983 were foreigners, many of whom returned home, the American problem multiplies. Of a total of 22,000 advanced degrees in engineering, probably half were to foreigners. To make matters more uncomfortable, the US is behind West Germany and Japan in engineering graduates per capita. The Japanese graduate about twice as many per capita as the US.

The lure of money has seduced many of the young into law and finance. In 1983 the US granted 37,000 law degrees, mostly to Americans. Thus, the US produces law degrees at about four times the rate that it produces advanced engineering degrees. This situation has resulted from the normal workings of a market process. It is mainly through the government expenditure of research money that science and engineering are stimulated. Without a national commitment to expanding scientific and engineering training, the market will continue to dominate the allocation of students.

Increasing Investment in New Technology
The most important factor in enhancing productivity advancement is the overall level of investment in new plant and equipment. It is through this process that new technology is introduced and old technology is extended. The government directly contributes to this process through its responsibility for maintaining the social infrastructure of roads, waterways, airports and other productive facilities. In the past decade, government investment in these facilities has declined relative to overall investment. It must be increased to further the growth in new technology, presumably at the expense of government-sponsored consumption. This is a problem not only for the federal government, but for state and local governments as well.

Private investment as a percentage of GNP varies significantly over the business-cycle, falling in recessions and rising in expansions. Stabilizing the economy is the single most important factor in maintaining the absolute level of investment. This, of course, raises the heated debate over activist versus stable predictable policies. There are certain critical historical moments when activist policy is essential, e.g. 1934 and 1982. One should not be doctrinaire on these matters. In a paraphrase from a famous Beatles song, the market sometimes needs a little help from its friends. In most periods, however, a stable, predictable government monetary and fiscal environment is needed.

In the proper aggregate demand environment, the level of investment will depend on the rate of technological advance. Not unlike the destructive effects of war, new technology obsoletes old technology and gives rise to a need for more investment. Along with aggregate demand, this consideration is far more important than the real interest rate in determining the rate of investment.

There are other policies besides either monetary and fiscal policy or educational policy whereby the government can influence the rate of technological change. America's advances in computer and aerospace technology owe much to military investment in research and development in these areas, especially in the 1950s and 1960s.

At the present time, military R & D is about 30 per cent of total government and private R & D in the United States. The military continues to support heavily developments in computers and materials. A much smaller level government support comes from NASA, NSF and other government agencies. Small pre-commerical research programmes exist in the Bureau of Standards and the Department of Energy. Total government support for computer research and development is absolutely large although only about 5 per cent of overall government support for R & D. This does not include tax credits for private research and development.

There is some mention of establishing a National Office of Technology, one capable of monitoring domestic and international technology developments, facilitating joint government – industry research ventures, and subsidizing private research efforts in pre-commercial activities. The budget for this agency would of necessity be large and it would appropriately replace the Department of Defense research activities that are not of a purely military nature. By directly pursuing commercial advantage rather than treating it as a by-product of military research efforts, a more efficient expenditure of funds might be anticipated.

However, in the current American political environment, federal support of commercial R & D would be buffeted by the forces of special interest politics that has now so completely stalemated the American polity. The United States could not currently have a rational, far-sighted programme in search of international technological advantage. Thus the only practical way to provide government support for technological advance is through the budget of the Department of Defense. Given that there are good reasons for believing that the social returns from research and development exceed the private returns, and that the market provides too little of this activity, some government support, however indirect and costly, is probably better than nothing.

NOTES

1. I would like to thank Kenneth Flamn of the Brookings Institution for his insights into computer technology and especially his understanding of the capabilities and employment of industrial robots.

REFERENCES

Becker, Gary. *Human Capital* (Chicago: University of Chicago Press, 1964).
Flamn, Kenneth. *Targeting the Computer* (Washington, DC: Brookings Institution, 1987).
Flamn, Kenneth. *Creating the Computer: Government Industry and High Technology* (Washington, DC: Brookings Institution, 1988).
Griliches, Zvi. *R & D, Patents and Productivity* (Chicago: University of Chicago Press, 1984).
Simon, Herbert A. *Administrative Behavior* (New York: Free Press, 1976).
Solow, Robert M. 'Technical Change and the Aggregate Production Function' *Review of Economics and Statistics* (1957), **3**, pp. 312-20.

3 Productivity and Workplace Organization*

INTRODUCTION

The current economic and social difficulties of the industrialized nations, indeed of the entire world economy, can be studied from a variety of perspectives. One can study slow output growth, or high unemployment, or excessive inflation, or the difficulty of adapting to changing relative oil and grain prices, or the increase in the real price of gold, or the weakening Soviet and US alliance systems, or declining productivity. Ultimately, these problems are all reflections of the same complex set of underlying causes – international monetary disorder, commerical conflict, changing military and political alliances, and the breakdown of domestic political and moral authority. In this context, one of serious economic and social dislocation, I shall consider certain aspects of the worker participation movement in the United States over the past decade. Of primary concern will be the problem of interface between this movement and technological developments.

A study of this interrelationship provides an opportunity to examine the issue of worker participation in the dynamic context of technological change, a process which includes not just the introduction of machine-embodied inventions, but changes in both the physical arrangements and the social relations of the workplace. This broader concept of technological change simplifies thinking about the way in which culture as embodied in workplace organization either facilitates or blocks change. It also makes it easier to comprehend why, once begun, change may encounter a

*Written in the winter of 1981–82

54

rigid social system, one which fails to adapt to the physical and organizational requirements of a new technology.

WORKER PARTICIPATION AND ECONOMIC GROWTH

A successful worker-participation movement will affect the organization of the workplace. In the writings of Braverman, Simon and others, it is understood that workplace organization is an important part of the productivity puzzle. To this extent it will also affect the effectiveness of new machines and new methods, and their productivity as defined by a unit of capital's contribution to national product. All new machines and techniques must, of course, be embedded in the context of the workplace, a production and distribution arrangement where the mechanical interface between people and machines – the so-called 'classical' view of production – as well as interaction among people – the so-called 'human relations' aspect of production – takes place. Any effort to accumulate capital without first achieving labour flexibility runs the risk of this capital being either underutilized or inappropriately applied. Flexibility is achieved by means of either labour's co-operation or labour's submission.

Of course, the organization of the workplace only partly defines the problem of economic growth. Growth also requires a high savings rate combined with the desire and ability of large corporations to utilize these savings effectively. However, when oil and other energy sources are costly, or when resources are fully employed, or when there is some other barrier to growth, there will be a constraint on total output. In this instance, an increased savings rate means a reduced consumption rate. This will place a limit on real wages. Moreover, even if these constraints are relaxed, there might still remain limits on real wages because of increasing import competition.

Understandably, then, it might be difficult to organize the workplace on the basis of an arrangement whereby workers are motivated to cooperate in production by means of high wages, and correspondingly, comfortable consumption. There is a potential problem of motivation here, for wage incentive systems are motivational arrangements with which Americans are quite familiar. Their importance was appreciated fully by such pragmatic men as James Couzens, a Henry Ford associate who, before World War I, first proposed the Five Dollar Day. Farm boys and others responded with much enthusiasm to the prospect of economic advancement. Wage incentives were used to motivate workers during and after World War II. In both of these periods, it was the promise and reality of mass consumption which motivated and activated the productive capacity inherent in the cognitive and physical skills of the American people.

Not only must savings be invested, they must be invested productively. The Japanese economic miracle, for example, would not have occurred had not the Japanese *keiretsu*, in conjunction with the Ministry of International Trade and Industry, wisely chosen to develop first shipbuilding and steel capacity, then chemical-producing capacity, and then an automobile industry capable of producing fuel-efficient automobiles. Similarly, the American economic miracle would never have occurred without the development of the efficient nineteenth-century steel industry or the highly mechanized agricultural sector. At the other extreme, the recent waste of funds in the construction of high-rise office buildings and shopping malls in the United States, or the excessive application of borrowed foreign funds to construct public facilities in the Germany of the 1920s, or the overbuilding of the American railroad system in the nineteenth century, were all unhappy instances of savings being squandered in unproductive investments.

An efficiently organized workplace, adequate savings and productive outlets for these savings are not a complete list of the preconditions for economic expansion. The supporting institutions of the society – the family, the church, the community and the government – must all be respected and have the confidence of people. In the broadest sense, this requires that the system of laws, customs and beliefs be one which fosters peace, a general popular feeling of social justice and equity, and a respect for hard work.

JAPANESE AND AMERICAN GROWTH STYLES

The preceding discussion of the issues relating to workplace organization might seem somewhat technocratic, for it ignores the political dimension of change. While the growth process requires a *modus operandi* for the workplace, it is probably impossible and, indeed, even inadvisable, to adopt a single approach to the problem of workplace organization in a nation as socially, ethnically and racially diverse as the United States. In such situations, however, it might be practical to have a nationally or regionally dominant approach.

Americans could develop and, under proper circumstances,

introduce elements of the Japanese system of workplace organization. After all, there are some very close similarities between the organization of the Japanese workplace and American military organization, especially with respect to the role of authority and loyalty as organizing principles. However, it would be neither possible nor desirable to import the Japanese factory system into the United States. Brady, Dore and others describe a paternalistic system which is an integral part of a wider cultural system in which not only the factory but the schools, the family and the broader community are influenced and driven by historical and institutional imperatives reflected in people's attitudes. Japanese culture supports groupishness and a respect for age, authority and work which is reflected in the workplace through a system of work assignments, 'lifetime' employment, and internal wage differentials. In turn, the large Japanese corporation is itself part of a broader financial and industrial planning system without which the implementation of guaranteed employment would be impractical. Without such planning, it would be difficult to maintain the domestic or foreign markets upon which is based their employment guarantees.

As described by Arrow, Simon and Weber, there is much variation in the authority systems governing the organization of the workplace. In the United States, there are three historically distinct methods of management and factory workplace organization. In the years of rapid industrial expansion following the Civil War the workplace was rather harshly organized with the extensive use of straw bosses, expediters, supervisors and overseers. There followed a long period – from the turn of the century through the 1920s – of machine-paced work coupled with Taylorism and the rationalization of work associated with these ideas. The fragmentation of tasks and the extreme specialization of work, common features of assembly operations, were emerging in the years before World War I. They were perfected in the open shop years of the 1920s. The methods generated boring and repetitive work. By the same token, it was very productive, and even Lenin argued for its introduction in Soviet factories in 1918. These techniques enabled manufacturers to reduce prices. In 1908 the first Model T sold for $1500: in 1915 for $400!

With the advent of CIO unionism, there came another long period during which workers were machine-paced. But now authority in the workplace was tempered by collective bargaining. In this arrangement, many employment conditions were subject to negotiation. In the manufacturing, mining and transportation sectors of the American economy – the unionized sectors – this unique American-style workplace arrangement developed. It was the American counterpart of the Japanese system, but one supported by coalition politics rather than custom and habit. Workers were tied to the corporations through the 'cash nexus'. High wages which supported comfortable consumption provided the motivation or at least the willingness of men and women to exert effort and to subject themselves to machine pacing. Their unions, through a process of government-sponsored collective bargaining – a process facilitated by such regulatory agencies as the National Labor Relations Board, the Railway Labor Boards, and the Interstate Commerce Commission – significantly influenced the social relations of the workplace. They did so by negotiating and enforcing seniority systems and grievance procedures. In the first instance age and time of service were formalized as the bases for job security. In the latter instance the rule of law with its accompaniment of precedence and arbitrators was introduced to adjudicate disputes.

Because of these developments, the social relations of the workplace were set not only by the technology embodied in machines – e.g. the continuous flow process of a chemical facility or the assembly-line process of a facility producing durable goods – but by a coalition between workers and managers. This coalition was stable as long as economic growth continued and so long as both parties were unwilling to sustain a strike for too long. Their common cause in the process of production overrode their inherent antagonisms. Under these conditions it is not surprising that many organizational theorists like Cyert and March developed coalition theories of organizations, while economists like Hicks developed theoretical models which implied strikes of short duration and which were most appropriate for the muted conflict of this period, not for, say, the 1919 steel strike, the 1920 French railway strike, or the 1981 air traffic controllers' strike.

In this collective bargaining system seniority provisions which governed layoffs, transfers and promotions provided protection and job security not too dissimilar from the often-praised Japanese 'lifetime' employment system. When coupled with both the commitment to a rule of law and with a national Social Security system, one can only conclude that for the 20 per cent of the labour force employed in heavy industry, a system as protective as the Japanese system existed in the United States. Although the American system progressively had been weakening during the 1970s, it was not until the 1979–80 collapse in car sales that the system ruptured with ramifications throughout the closely interconnected midwestern industrial complex.

It should be emphasized that this description does not apply to those workers who were concentrated in service, sales and office work, who were professionals, who were civil servants, or who were undocumented workers from around the world. In these instances, workplace organization was vastly different from the unionized sector of heavy industry.

Now that the workplace must be reconstituted there is the political question of whether management will seek a friendly accommodation with labour – both organized and unorganized – or whether it will attempt a reinstitution of an earlier system in which labour can be viewed in machine terms and in which it can be made to accommodate change by the harsher methods of supervisory control and the threat of dismissal. On the other hand, the worker participation movement is an effort at accommodation by some employers. Of course, we should not ignore the unpleasant fact that many employers may try to use the movement to undermine unions or to brainwash workers.

THE WORKER-PARTICIPATION MOVEMENT

For the past fifteen years a variety of worker-participation programmes – sometimes labelled 'work-restructuring', 'job-enrichment' or 'quality-of-worklife' programmes – have been introduced, primarily in large corporations, primarily at management initiative, and primarily on an experimental basis. In this process, much has been learned about workplace group dynamics, individual motivation and labour participation arrangements. In some small way, these efforts reverse the 'scientific management' movement which was designed to remove responsibility for planning from the shopfloor and then to plan each task in the most minute detail.

The Taylorist movement was based on several assumptions concerning the appropriate method for organizing work in order to maximize output per hour worked. Melman and others have described this method. The required tasks were constantly simplified by subdividing them into smaller and smaller components. Work assignments were correspondingly reduced in complexity. These assignments were unvarying, requiring workers to perform repetitively the same simple tasks. Skill was defined in terms of the requirements of the machine. Skills were thought of in manual/manipulative rather than cognitive terms. Production work and decision-making work were separated.

Many technologies clearly required this routinization of human activity. Others did not. However, Taylorization became a widely employed system of factory workplace organization. Other potentially productive arrangements were excluded. In human activities it is not always the best or optimal technique of organization that is adopted. Often a satisfactory technique catches hold and spreads. Once adopted, it is not easily displaced. Meanwhile, other and sometimes even better techniques remain undiscovered. This is behaviour defined by the requirements of 'bounded rationality' or 'satisficing', ideas that Simon has developed. Unlike the economist's notion of maximizing, which assumes that we are always in the best of all possible worlds, they allow for improving on existing social and economic institutions.

The machine view of labour has it obvious limitations. Workers can frustrate the efforts of management either individually or collectively. They can disrupt production by breaking machinery, by absenteeism, by varying the pace of work, by circumventing rules, or by disobeying instructions. The voluntary compliance of workers is obviously desirable, but not always achievable. Sometimes, however, by giving workers status and responsibility, management may gain their loyalty and instill enthusiasm. This would permit capitalizing on the superior adaptability of labour as compared to machines.

Such a strategy has been called 'responsible autonomy'. It is to be distinguished from the strategy of direct control of which Taylorism or 'scientific management' is an important instance. The introduction of worker-participation systems does not entail a drastic transformation of corporate governance, and these efforts should not be confused with movements for industrial democracy or worker self-management as described by Vanek.

The current effort to reverse the Taylorist movement and enlist the voluntary support of workers is stimulated partly by a desire to enhance productivity. It is presumed that by involving workers or their representatives in workplace issues, workers will be motivated and their motivation will contribute to a smoother functioning and more effective workplace. The relationship between participation and motivation should not be overstressed, however. Many workers would gladly participate in the design of more fragmented work if it meant higher wages. Meaningful work is only one of many human objectives. In many circumstances, it is not always the most important.

Recently, Nelson cast a sceptical note concerning the productivity-enhancing effects of worker-participation experiments. In his summary of the literature on these experiments he finds that while students of human relations and social organization have effectively buried the machine view of business organization, they have not been able to identify stable relationships between worker-participation-type control variables and worker performance. I do not find this result especially surprising.

In the famous 1958 March–Simon study it is convincingly argued that the relationship between motivation and performance is complex. My own reading of their work suggests that it is so complex that it defies useful abstraction and generalization. This is not to deny the usefulness of viewing the process in complex terms. For example, the study of social relations in the framework of complex flowchart or simultaneous differential equation models sometimes provides the investigator with useful insights into the situation under examination. Some understanding of a particular work situation can be achieved if complex models are viewed as organizing or bookkeeping devices, not as scientific abstractions useful for predictive purposes.[1]

It is not difficult to explain why a stress on worker motivation has become increasingly a matter of corporate concern in recent years. In many human activities psychological factors, indeed even chance, are important determinants of behaviour and outcome. Yet, their importance is often forgotten or taken for granted, especially when this neglect does not lead to individual or organizational ruin. However, at critical historical moments, failure to recognize these qualitative aspects of human interaction is potentially ruinous. The current period is just such an historical moment.

History is replete with reminders of this lesson. Chance is used by Tolstoy to 'explain' the unwise decision of France to invade Russia. Clausewitz, on the other hand, stresses the importance of loyalty and morale for success in military endeavours. The Prussian armies, despite their mechanical coordination, their close order manoeuvrability, and their professional officer corps, were decimated by the Napoleonic armies driven by unparalleled revolutionary and nationalistic fervour. Clausewitz learned many lessons from the Prussian failures, not least of which was the idea that armies are not machines. They are groups of men requiring coordination and discipline. Naturally, like all human organizations, they are subject to human emotions and the uncertainties of human interaction. This reality must be constantly emphasized, lest it be forgotten.[2]

ADAPTING TO TECHNICAL CHANGE

Much of the literature on worker participation proceeds independently of the literature on technological change. In a context of either slowly advancing technology or fixed technology, Taylorism, the continuous fragmentation of tasks, is pitted against worker participation which to various degrees attempts to reverse job fragmentation. However, the comparison is more profitably considered in terms of the interpersonal and other social arrangements of the workplace which are necessary to accommodate and facilitate the introduction of new methods and machines.

It is important to recognize that even within the existing configuration of technologies it is sometimes possible to redesign the workplace in the direction of more, not less, complex tasks, more not less complex assignments, varying not fixed work assignments, the interface rather than separation of manual and intellectual skills, and the intertwining rather than separating of production and decision-making work. Nor should it be assumed that such redesign would be unproductive. Even in the machine-paced process of the automobile assembly-line, there are opportunities for redesigning the work process in more interesting and challenging directions without a loss of productivity.

It should not be surprising that these opportunities exist. It would be a remarkable accident if the introduction and development of Fordism had hit on the best or optimal arrangement of jobs on an assembly-line. Once Ford and his imitators uncovered satisfactory levels of efficiency, workplace redesign slowed considerably. As described by Abernathy, the small changes that did take place, continued to embody the principle of continuous fragmentation. Perhaps worker-participation systems simply recognize that a good thing was carried too far.

Turning to new technologies, there are sometimes opportunities to vary their design so that they interface with workers in varying ways. All technologies do not develop according to an inevitable historical logic. Some do not necessitate the continuous division of labour. Technology results, at least in part, from social choice. When there is choice among technologies, the alternative that is chosen will depend on the political and social situation in the society. Some choices involve the further division of labour, others do not.

Many commerical technologies were borrowed from the military. Their associated social relations in commercial applications were therefore determined by military decisions which, in turn, were based on difficult judgements about how an untried technology would perform in future and therefore uncertain battlefield conditions. In many instances, one can imagine different military decisions which would have significantly altered the character of the borrowed technology. I have in mind the commercial application of nuclear power, the commercial introduction of jumbo jets, the commerical application of containerization, and the commercial development of numerically-controlled machine tools. In each of these instances, one could systematically trace out different scenarios in which the commercial application of the technology would have different impacts on the division of labour, authority relations at the workplace, or other aspects of workplace social relations.[3] Unfortunately, it is difficult to establish the quantitative relevance of these considerations.

ECONOMIC RESTRUCTURING AND WORKER PARTICIPATION

It is in the nature of new technology and new ways of doing things that flexibility is required. The process of trial and error – constant rearrangement, rescheduling, relabelling, redoing, remaking – is essential to the learning process. A new technique, a new process, a new organizational structure, all require the acquisition of not only new mechanical skills but new organizational and social skills. In part, this will undoubtedly involve the redesign and relayout of existing workplaces but it will more importantly involve the restructuring of attitudes and organizational arrangements to facilitate the introduction of new machinery, new products and new technologies.

The introduction of new technology is usually a process, not an event. It takes time for individuals and working groups to learn and adapt to new technology. New machines, new plans and new designs infrequently define the required task so restrictively as to preclude the need for continuous re-evaluation, redesign and rearrangement. Initially, there is always room to manoeuvre, to search and to learn. It is within the framework of these broad limits that 'learning-by-doing' occurs, both for individuals and work groups. In time, of course, the limits narrow and productivity gains diminish, eventually reaching a steady state.

Although the movement for worker participation pre-dated the clear necessity to restructure the American ecomony, it is none the less fruitfully analysed in the framework of these requirements. The organization of the workplace must accommodate the introduction of new technology and the development of social relations consistent with the productive development and extension of that technology. It is understood that the body rejects foreign elements. Likewise, the social system rejects those technologies which ignore its cultural and political imperatives.

The growing effort to introduce new information technology in the service of routine and programmable tasks, an effort at both the factory and the office, is a development which will transform the organization of the workplace. Only the barest outlines of this transformation are now clear. This uncertainty exists in part because the direction of these organizational changes is not fully predetermined by the technology, for the technology is not yet fully developed in the hardware sense nor is its configuration and operating mode fully determined in a software sense. There is room to manoeuvre, there is space, and the possibility exists for the participation of labour in the implementation process. Labour might to some limited extent – or perhaps even to considerable extent – shape the final configuration of the technological future of the factory and office. However, without some degree of real worker power through disciplined union organization, one might question the true potential for the worker-participation movement to help guide the reorganization of work and to facilitate the introduction of new technology.

THE ASSEMBLY-LINE REVOLUTION

This dynamic process of introducing new technology is readily appreciated in the historical development of the moving assembly-line. Mass production techniques were not simply introduced into the automobile industry, but rather they evolved slowly over the period 1910–15. With a machine view of workers and with a relatively malleable workforce, Ford and his engineers constantly reorganized the various departments of the Ford Motor Company. Straight-line production required the orderly arrangement of equipment in parallel lines, rather than their arrangement by class of machinery: lathes together, power-drills together, and so forth. There followed the introduction of 'moving assembly' on feeder routes, then to the final line. In time a 'moving assembly' changed from crude gravity-slides to a continuous automative conveyor-belt. To borrow a metaphor from Keith Sward, the production line resembled a river and its tributaries.

By 1915, this new mass-production technique was a far cry from the shop of 1908 in which the first Model T was built. Then a versatile mechanic assembled an automobile together using a stationary technology. Subsequently a highly subdivided task was assigned to a worker who was to engage in a dull and repetitive task over an entire working life. Needless to say, turnover was high – 40–60 per cent per month. To cope with this problem, Ford adopted the strategy of high wages – the Five Dollar Day. This mitigated but did not end the industry's intense labour problems.

High wages and associated high consumption served to motivate labour and create discipline and high productivity during the decade after World War I and again for three decades after World War II. However, as the decade of the Great Depression demonstrates, high wages – and they were high during that period, at least for those who had work – must be coupled with high employment, otherwise job insecurity will destabilize the workplace. For those who doubt this proposition, recall the unprecedented increase in the extent of union militancy during the years 1934–37.

In the present period, constraints on the availability of reasonably priced oil and import competition limit the possibility of adopting a high-wage strategy to motivate work. Continuing problems of motivation, absenteeism and productivity suggest that the current shortage of jobs serves only to increase anxiety and not in some classic Austrian or Marxian reserve army sense to increase labour discipline and productivity. It would appear that the labour force is being demoralized, not 'whipped into shape'. Furthermore, if the 1930s experience is any indication of future possibilities, an increase in the unemployment rate from the current 7 or 8 per cent levels to the 10–20 per cent levels of that period is an invitation to social disorder and conflict, not to enhanced productivity.

It is difficult to escape the conclusion that there is a need for some mechanism other than unrestrained consumption to motivate work and reorganize industry. The 'threat of the sack' doesn't seem to help. It is the search for a new mechanism that informs the thinking of more thoughtful players in the worker-participation movement in America.

THE INFORMATION REVOLUTION

The moving assembly-line was a remarkable achievement. It represented a highly efficient substitution of mechanical energy for human energy. As Simon has stressed, the substitution process was the essence of the mechanistic-Newtonian approach to earning a living, an approach which constitutes an important dimension of the Industrial Revolution. This process of substitution was facilitated by a machine view of labour. We may now be entering the information revolution, the essence of which is the substitution of information by means of computer and other electronic technology for both mechanical and human energy.

The quantitative impact of these developments is potentially very large. A Carnegie–Mellon study states that upwards of one million factory jobs – assemblers, packagers, inspectors, welders, etc. – might be affected by these developments. In another study it is estimated that of the 3.5 million offices in the United States, 1.5 million are considered large enough for office automation. All such estimates must of course be viewed as speculative. Properly forewarned, note that in the factory it is mostly men who are affected; in the office, mostly women.

The human relations view, not the machine view, of workers and the workplace might best facilitate the successful introduction of this new technology. The current prominence of the human relations approach comes out of the humanistic values which are embedded in the institutions of the recent era. But it is important also because the concept of information as a productive input – productive in the same sense as human and machine energy – stems from the role which information plays in coordinating people who are pursuing common goals within an organization. Unlike machine discipline, which instills in people a mechanical cause-and-effect view of life, information often lacks the machine's repetitive precision. To be productive, information must combine with individual or collective judgement. In this instance, the workplace – and here I refer to the office, not the factory, for it is in the office that information technology will probably have its most profound effects – might best be viewed in human relations terms.

This argument does not deny that past mechanization and automation has routinized the jobs of workers in the lower strata nor is it meant to deny that it has tended to reduce personal contact on the job for these workers. Rather, it is an effort to indentify the possible limits of job routinization and depersonalization. Since both mechanization and automation apply to structured work, these limits are set by the pool of structured tasks which exist and those unstructured tasks that can be structured. Admittedly, the boundary between structured and structurable work, and unstructured work is vague. Nevertheless, there is a large pool of structurable tasks for which technology applies. In these instances, the technology is facilitating, not dehumanizing or deskilling. This optimistic view does not necessarily obviate the need for high or rising wages to motivate work. However, whether high wages will be as necessary in the office as they were in the factory remains highly uncertain.

CONCLUSIONS

When workers are insecure, when their workplace, their schools and their communities are in disarray, when their future, and especially the future of their children, is cloudy, then it is not surprising that they are poorly motivated, indeed even demoralized. What is needed is a sense of hope, a sense that they can build a better tomorrow for themselves and their children. It is obvious that the first order of business is to reconstitute a sense of community, both at work and in the neighbourhoods. At a minimum this requires a general feeling of security coupled with the knowledge that, regardless of economic vicissitudes, decent housing, decent clothing and decent food, as well as meaningful and effective education for the children, are available. These of course are nothing more than the minimum requirements of a decent state.

The issue of workplace reorganization is currently prominent because the American economy must be restructured in order to achieve the successful introduction of new technology. The threat of dismissal coupled with a machine view of labour were important elements in an earlier era of rapid accumulation. Later, it was high wages that motivated work and effort. It is now maintained that there is some need to involve people in the reconstruction of both the workplace and the community. But this involvement must be meaningful. It must be consistent with democratic principles. Workers must have an effective mechanism for involving themselves in the process of workplace reorganization.

To the extent that participatory arrangements substitute for monetary incentives – and I think this possibility is limited – they will not be effective. Nor will they be effective without full employment. The threat of job loss debilitates labour. Its success also requires effective union organization, for without organization, workers lack the authority and power to articulate and defend their needs. Without rising wages, full employment and labour organization, workplace restructuring and the introduction of new technology – which might often involve a reduction in the number of jobs – is unlikely to be achieved through the process of labour participation. It is crucial that the supporters of participatory plans appreciate the necessary marriage between these limited forms of industrial democracy and the commitment to a fully employed economy, one in which labour is effectively organized and committed to democratic ideals.

NOTES

1. Similar remarks apply to the use of complex linear programming models in the study, for example, of optimal transport fleets for either lorries or aircraft. Indeed, one can go even further for the principle is also applicable when large-scale, simultaneous-equation models are built to describe or replicate an economy. In these instances, the model-builder learns a great deal about the system he/she is attempting to model. The model serves as a formal accounting system to keep track of variables and relationships. The danger or course is that both the model-builder and user will come to reify the model or that the model will be used inappropriately to provide scientific legitimacy for one side or the other in a political struggle. In the past several years the use of large-scale econometric models has been perverted in the service of political manipulation and propaganda. Needless to say, this is not the fault of those who originally conceived of this approach to economic forecasting.
2. There are, of course, many other interesting examples of historical instances where psychological factors were of central importance in accounting for political, social and military developments. For example, in the 1930s, the rise of the Third Reich led to a rich literature on the mass psychology of fascism and on the role of the irrational in human events.
3. In a related view, Marglin (1974) argues that in the early days of the British Industrial Revolution, the factory system and its associated division of labour is best understood as an effort to control labour and only incidentally as an effort to increase productivity.

REFERENCES

Abernathy, William J. *The Productivity Dilemma: Roadblock to Innovation in the Automobile Industry* (Baltimore: Johns Hopkins Press, 1978).
Arrow, Kenneth. *The Limits of Organization* (New York: W. W. Norton, 1974).
Brady, Robert A. *Business as a System of Power* (New York: Columbia University Press, 1943).
Braverman, Harry. *Labor and Monopoly Capital: The Degradation of Work in the Twentieth Century* (New York: Monthly Review Press, 1974).
Cyert, Richard M. and March, James G. *A Behavorial Theory of the Firm* (Englewood Cliffs, NJ: Prentice-Hall, 1963).
Dore, Ronald. *British Factory – Japanese Factory: The Origins of National Diversity in Industrial Relations* (Berkeley: University of California Press, 1973).
Hicks, John R. *The Theory of Wages* (2nd ed) (London:Macmillan, 1964).
March, James and Simon, Herbert. *Organizations* (New York: Wiley & Sons, 1958).

Marglin, Stephen A. 'What Do Bosses Do? The Origins and Functions of Hierarchy in Capitalist Production', *The Review of Radical Political Economics*, Vol. VI, No. 2 (Summer 1974).

Nelson, Richard R. 'Research on Productivity Growth and Productivity Differences: Dead Ends and New Departures' (Forthcoming, *Journal of Economic Literature*).

Rapping, Leonard A. 'A World War II Shipbuilding Production Function', *Review of Economics and Statistics* (February 1963).

Simon, Herbert. *Models of Man: Social and Rational* (New York: Wiley & Sons, 1957).

Simon, Herbert. 'What Computers Mean for Man and Society', *Science*, Vol. 195, pp. 1186-91.

Sward, Keith. *The Legend of Henry Ford* (New York: Atheneum, 1975).

Taylor, Frederick W. *The Principles of Scientific Management* (New York: Harper & Bros, 1911).

Vanek, Jaroslav. *The General Theory of Labor Managed Market Economies* (Ithaca, NY: Cornell University Press, 1970).

4 Bureaucracy, the corporation and economic policy*

INTRODUCTION

The United States economy finds itself in worsening difficulties. Economic restructuring is clearly needed. This set of tasks is made more complex by continued low-level resource utilization, loss of American world position, inflexible government and corporate bureaucracies, and growing economic and social inequality. The basic economic problems of this era are structural and institutional, like those of the twenty-year crisis between the two world wars. Excessive unemployment and economic stagnation have resulted from changes in the composition of demand, technology, relative prices, governmental anti-inflation efforts and international competitiveness. A viable national economic programme must adapt to the long-run changes in the price of oil, grain and other natural resources, and it must adjust to the new international economic, military and political situation, involving a less dominant role for America in the world economy. Replacement of old, obsolete plants, rapid innovation and technology; and a new and less energy-intensive life-style must be accommodated. This will require important institutions – government, corporations, communities, schools, families – to adapt and change. This essay is concerned with the prospects for change in only one of these institutions, the American corporation.

Fifty years ago Berle and Means (1932) indicated that production and distribution are primarily organized by large-scale corporate bureaucracies. These hierarchical social systems are coordinated

---

* Reprinted with permission from *Journal of Post Keynesian Economics*, Spring 1984.

internally by authority relationships which are more or less constrained by market realities. These institutions interact among themselves and with other institutions in a market context. Market exchanges are governed by pecuniary, legal and social considerations. It is in monopolized markets where social factors – e.g. friendship, visual familiarity and social class – receive the greatest weight. However, even in competitive markets the social parameters of exchange are crucial. Trust and confidence are often as important as the 'bottom line' in initiating market behaviour.

Desired changes require corporate bureaucracies to be motivated to act and capable of acting intelligently. Their actions should be coordinated through the market system in a tolerably efficient manner. To encourage investment and innovation, national economic policy must manipulate those factors in the external environment which influence these institutions, and/or it must eliminate internal organizational arrangements which block innovation and change. In this light one should study the effects of monetarism, supply-side economics and industrial policy.

MONETARISM, SUPPLY-SIDE ECONOMICS AND INDUSTRIAL POLICY

Monetarism is supposedly the policy of sound money. Permitting a market-induced restriction of credit or initiating the restriction of credit, the central bank supposedly copes with the speculative excesses of an overexuberant expansion by creating unemployment and excess capacity. The ensuing struggle for financial survival is assumed to rekindle the old virtues of frugality, hard work and self-discipline. The weak are eliminated. The strong survive. Corporations and other social systems, not unlike individuals, are coerced in this process. Confronted with declining markets, these institutions are expected to eliminate waste and inefficiency, to reorganize the decision-making process and to proceed forward. Otherwise they will fail. The idea underlying this Darwinian process is summarized best in the motto of a 1930s advertising executive 'Progress Through Adversity'.

Of course, in this approach to restructuring corporate and other institutions in society, financial panic and collapse are ever-present risks. Firms and families might be immobilized by adversity. The corporation as a social system might disintegrate, not restructure, under adversity.[1]

Moreover, at a time when there is excessive corporate, consumer and government debt – not to mention Third World international debt – market contraction can trigger financial panic as cashflow problems develop (Minsky, 1975). The financial authorities must walk a tightrope between their tight money efforts and their lender-of-last-resort responsibilities. The outcome of this risky balancing act remains uncertain although the prospects for success are not encouraging.

Supply-side economics, in its excessive and unfair tax-cutting incarnation during the early months of the Republican administration, can be interpreted charitably as an incentive economic programme, based on the belief that corporations are structurally sound, that they are capable of effective long-run decision-making, and that through the unfettered market process they would respond appropriately and in a coordinated fashion to pecuniary incentives. They would eliminate waste, invest in new techniques, discover new processes, products and markets, and create jobs and prosperity.

History's verdict on the recent incarnation of supply-side economics seems inevitable. Even if the element of greed and indiscretion in the 1981 tax cuts is ignored, it was a programme that failed to take account of the basic unsoundness of the current corporate bureaucratic structure and that failed to recognize the difficulties of an unregulated market system to effectively coordinate independent decision-making units.[2]

Can change be based on a national economic policy which achieves consensus and broad support? Support and consensus is facilitated by a programme which promises a fair allocation of the potential gains from economic stabilization and a not-too-uneven distribution of the discomfort which will inevitably accompany the retrenchment, readjustment, and reinvestment necessary to develop a new economic and social foundation for prosperity. Proponents of this view sometimes organize under the term 'industrial policy', a generic term calling for both public regulation and direction of market processes.[3] Industrial policy represents an effort to support financially potentially growing sectors, to coordinate corporate decision-making, and to ease social and economic adjustments in declining industries. Only to a limited extent is it an effort at parliamentary participation in internal corporate decision-making processes.[4] Government is necessary to reduce uncertainty which can paralyse decision-makers, to introduce an element of fairness into the adjustment process so as to minimize potential opposition to changes, and to protect the public against corporate decisions which calculate only private, not public, net advantage.

THE STRUCTURAL ROOTS OF ECONOMIC STAGNATION

An economic recovery programme must be based on theory – or even perhaps an idea or an inkling – concerning the causes of economic stagnation. There is no simple explanation for economic failure. Karl Marx argued that labour power was crucial to production. When labour was scarce, an economy would stagnate. This is not the problem in this economy, for there is abundant labour both at home and abroad.

The argument is common that scarce resources – land, oil, grain, and other raw materials – set limits to growth, thereby inducing economic conflict as owners of the scarce resources appropriate an increasing share of the social product. Since the early 1970s, the prices of grain, oil, and some other raw materials have skyrocketed. Many observers attribute this event to concentrated monopoly power in the southwestern United States and in the Middle East and not so much to the exhaustion of the earth's crust. In any event, these developments have intensified conflict globally – inflation is the monetary manifestation of this conflict. The resolution to the resource problem is usually sought in technology – meaning knowledge – and in innovation – meaning the application of knowledge – both of which can help in conserving scarce resources and in developing new energy sources.

Economic stagnation is sometimes seen as a failure of technology. In the 1930s it was popular to argue that innovative waves or technological revolutions were the forces behind long-term economic expansion. In this view, the innovation and innovator are crucial. Steampower in the early 1800s, railroads in the mid- and late 1800s, and electric power and the automobile in the 1920s were all instances of technology-driven expansions. In this view, economic survival is dependent on wits and common sense as embodied in science and technology.

Science and technology have postponed the gruesome biological tragedy anticipated by Malthus. But they have also given birth to nuclear bombs, launching the possibility of an equally gruesome nuclear tragedy. Despite this contradictory development, many American economists remain technological optimists and place great stress on technology as a source of growth and prosperity. While they stress the productivity-enhancing effects of machine-embodied innovations like the oxygen furnace, the diesel locomotive, the electronic computer and the jet engine, they also recognize that the visual concreteness of these technical innovations sometimes inappropriately rivets our attention on the machine rather than the social organization of production and the motivation of the individual.[5] On reflection, one cannot help but appreciate the productivity-enhancing importance of such organizational and intellectual innovations as the multidivisional firm described by Chandler (1977), 'scientific management' popularized by Taylor (1911), the social convention of using money and credit to circulate commodities to store wealth analysed by Keynes (1936), the assumption by Simon (1977) in the field of artificial intelligence that thought processes can be simulated on a computer, and the remarkable effort by Freud to think rationally about the irrational.

THE POST-WORLD WAR II PROSPERITY

While we must stress the technological base of the postwar prosperity, it would be narrow-minded to ignore cheap energy as well as supportive social arrangements, of which the domestic 'social contract' and the stable international monetary and commercial order that existed between 1945 and 1971 were most prominent and important.

The metalworking and agricultural sectors of the American economy were at this time very productive. In agriculture, manufacturing, mining and transportation, productivity advanced as oil-intensive machine power replaced people power. The surplus from these sectors supported expanded service and government sectors. White-collar employment in both the government and corporate bureaucracies grew rapidly. Service sector employment in such industries as eating and drinking places, banks and insurance companies also expanded.[6]

The long post-World War II expansion ended sometime in the early 1970s. Its conclusion necessitated the reconstruction and reorientation of the economy; but no consensus was reached on how to conserve and develop energy and other resources, how to restructure the lifestyle, how to relate to an emerging world situation attendant upon the end of the American system, or, in general, on how to proceed or where to go.

The Carter administration lacked the political power to recast and redirect the economy, for this would have entailed confronting an uncertain economic future with honesty and optimism. This could be done only if the society had confidence in itself and its future. Lacking sufficient political support, the Carter administration exercised the only politically feasible option: it finessed the problem by importing large amounts of oil and expanding credit. A mini-boom on the old consumption model followed. The 1976–79 American expansion supported a large part of a world economy that was dependent on American consumption spending for markets. One must appreciate that the Carter administration, by bolstering the United States and world economies, probably averted an economic calamity in the latter part of the 1970s. Indeed, in an important sense American economic policy over the entire decade of the 1970s was a success in the sense that it either prevented or delayed a second Great Depression.

THE NEW REPUBLICAN ADMINISTRATION

In 1981, the new administration embarked on a new economic programme. By tax-cutting, it wanted to increase the potential after-tax profitability of acquiring assets. They hoped to stimulate innovation, the replacement of old and obsolete plants and equipment, and the development and extension of new forward-looking industries and to promote the training and retraining of workers. In time – so the argument went – the standard of living would improve.

The hypothesis was that extraordinary profits would incite men and women of entrepreneurial cunning to innovate, create and solve the economic problems of our era. But production is organized largely by highly bureaucratic corporations; even entrepreneurs of enormous creativity and imagination would find it necessary to express and implement their ideas and plans in corporate offices and boardrooms. There they would be subjected to the customs, habits and traditions of the American corporate bureaucracy. In these bureaucracies individuality is suppressed.[7]

The administration's economic programme presumed that these institutions suffer neither from sclerosis nor from bureaucratic shortsightedness, and, moreover, they are better long-run planning instruments than federal bureaucracies. Unfortunately, American corporate bureaucracies, like their government counter-parts, must be restructured. In their current condition and frame of mind, increasing their retained earnings by tax cuts simply encouraged excessive executive compensation and corporate takeovers, mergers and acquisitions, rather than the innovation and creativity needed to develop new and useful products, new production techniques and new ideas on conserving energy and other scarce resources.

MANAGING IN TIMES OF HIGH COST INPUTS

Over the past hundred years the expanding American economy has benefited from a variety of fortunate geographic, geological and political circumstances. Until recently it had abundant and cheap energy – first wood, then coal, then oil – and manpower. American economic growth was fashioned in a psychological and physical environment of never-ending supply. Except in the years after World War II when satisfying foreign markets occupied both foreign and US producers, these opportunities were protected for American business by tariff policy. The skills necessary to exploit these frontiers and opportunities in an era of plenty are different from the skills necessary to survive in a world in which the global frontiers and markets are contracting, in which the rule is high cost rather than cheap inputs and increasing demand, and in which competition has greatly increased.

In an environment of plenty, Americans have glorified efforts at personal economic success. American management has historically been pragmatic and rational in pursuing its economic objectives. Relatively unfettered by custom, tradition and sentimentally, it has been instrumental, experimental and willing to take risks. In an environment of abundance and rapidly growing markets, this risk-taking has often yielded handsome returns. However, under current circumstances, the payoffs may well be smaller than they used to be and managerial attitudes and values must be changed. Management has been encouraged by a more competitive and difficult environment with slowly growing markets to seek pecuniary advantage in finance and marketing rather than in production. This is not a promising development, especially when an economy must be restructured – an inherently risky task.

DEVELOPING BUREAUCRACIES

The long post-World War II expansion submerged the individuality, initiative and discretion of many managers into corporate and government bureaucracies. These bureaucracies developed as a rational response to problems of managing a global system. Bureaucracy is a useful way of utilizing human skills in the imperfect form in which they exist. When an organization's objectives are stable and clearly defined, when the means of success are well understood, and when the future is seen as little more than an extrapolation of the past, bureaucracy is a useful organizational arrangement for routinizing problem-solving and minimizing the need for discretion and initiative. Even change itself is sometimes programmed. In bureaucratic organizations, efficiency, change and continued success are possible provided the problems of tomorrow will not be too dissimilar from the problems of today. But when the environment changes significantly, as it has in recent years, bureaucracies bound by fixed routines and encrusted interests are sometimes incapable of responding to new challenges.[8] Management becomes dysfunctional. This point is made by Peter Drucker (1980), who argues that in 'predictable times' fundamentals can be ignored but in 'turbulent times' they must be managed.

In the post-World War II years two bureaucracies developed in the United States. Federal government departments and bureaus multiplied, while corporate divisions, branches and subsidiaries proliferated at home and abroad. Bureaucratization increased as efforts were made to rationalize both corporate and federal government structures. The business schools were imporant vehicles for training the corporate managers, while schools of public administration grew up to rationalize the public bureaucracies. Management techniques and ideas were exchanged between these bureaucracies, on both a formal and an informal basis. Shared ideology, shared educational experience, shared world views, and shared interests bound these bureaucracies together in thought and deed.

The similarities in experience and organization between public and private bureaucracies would lead to some doubt as to whether it is appropriate to describe free enterprise as flexible, enterprising, motivated and pragmatic, while describing government as apathetic, discouraged, impractical and tired. Perhaps these adjectives seem appropriate when one compares, say, IBM to some of the tired and besieged state governments on the eastern seaboard. But they are not especially appropriate when comparing Metropolitan Edison, Chrysler, Lockheed, the old Penn Central, or the Penn Square Bank to such successful federal agencies as the pre-Reagan Environmental Protection Agency or the National Institutes of Health.

Economists of conservative or New Right persuasion sometimes suggest that the difference between private and public bureaucracies is the profit motive, which incites private seekers of pecuniary success to efforts and achievements unparalleled by their public counterparts. But with environmental and workplace pollution – what economists call externalities – current prices which determine profits are no longer reliable guides. Moreover, an uncertain future makes future prices, which also determine profits, uncertain and in principle unknowable. Consequently, current or prospective accounting profits can no longer guide the investment process in an efficient and socially beneficial way. Corporate bureaucracies can and do make decisions; but there should be no presumption that these decisions are in some different efficiency domain from the decisions of government bureaucracies.

Nor will bankruptcy eliminate the inefficient private bureaucracies. With the economy dominated by large corporations interlocked with other corporations in product markets in which they are demanders from and suppliers to each other, and in financial markets in which they are borrowers from and lenders to each other, large corporate failures are almost impossible. And these failures are not allowed for good reason. In these unstable times, a series of failures could reverberate through product and financial markets, causing other failures and perhaps financial panic. Even in earlier years, when the potential for interlocking disaster was considerably smaller, large corporations rarely failed.

THE QUANTITATIVE WORLDVIEW

The professionalization of the corporate and federal government managerial class was achieved through formal schooling in which modern management techniques played an important role. These techniques were taught in an effort to introduce scientific method, or, to use a less formal phrase 'straight thinking', into the training of managers. Simon (1976) stresses that this professionalization of management was simply an extension of the scientific management movement. In addition, because of World War II development of both operations research and the modern electronic computer, modern management training was enmeshed in quantitative techniques to a greater extent than earlier. A similar explosion of mathematical technique occurred in other areas like economics. In management training a variety of quantitative methods were introduced – linear and dynamic programming, probability models, inventory, marketing and production models, economic discounting, marginal analysis and cost-benefit analysis. In increasing numbers, the modern middle-level manager was imbued with a quantitative worldview (or if not imbued, at least firmly pointed in that direction).

This quantitative view has its place and purpose. It is a useful guide to solving problems which are amenable to a programmed resolution. In this approach there is required a careful definition of purposes or ends, what economists and mathematicians call the objective function, the arguments of which are usually quantified by attaching dollar magnitudes to possible outcomes. It also requires mathematical abstraction to build a model of the system under investigation, one which captures enough of reality to be useful. It then requires parameter estimates for the model. This necessitates a reasonably stable environment because the past is usually used as a guide to parameter values in the future.[9]

A quantitative approach to business decision-making leads naturally although not necessarily, to excessive attention to measurable short-term accounting profits. Some suggest that the problem of American corporate decision-making is that it maximizes short, not long-run, profitability. Too much attention is given to measurable, immediate returns, to instant gratification, while too little attention is given to the uncertain and distant future. There is some basis for this contention. Too much of American managerial talent has been devoted to exploiting existing markets by manipulative marketing strategies, to corporate portfolio management which uses techniques designed to make money with money, and to the development of merger and other takeover strategies. Far too little energy has been devoted to production problems and process development, R & D, and strategic planning. In the words of Abernathy and Hayes (1980), 'The conclusion is powerful and must be faced .... They (American managers) have abdicated their strategic responsibilities.'

The effectiveness of quantitative decision-making for long-run choices has been lessened because the time horizon over which measurement is feasible has contracted. Now, only the present and not too distant future are subject to numerical description. This state of affairs has resulted from many developments which have disrupted confidence in the future and weakened or destroyed the usefulness or useability of prices, which are important in quantification. Inflation threatens almost everywhere, there are major global political changes, populations are on the move, war is frequent, and the threat of large-scale war is all too real.

To borrow a metaphor from Kenneth Arrow, the successful use of quantitative approaches depends heavily on the receipt and interpretation of signals from the price system. The wage rate and the prices of oil, food, transportation services, taxes and other important items must be stable and predictable. Otherwise they could not be used for planning purposes and certainly cannot be inputs into a mathematical model. Moreover, these prices have to index or measure something about which we are concerned. Thus, for example, if price increases are to motivate conservation, the rising prices should index physical scarcities, not monopoly or other social contrivances.

There are two other important situations in which prices are imprecise and unreliable signals. First, so-called externalities – e.g. environmental and workplace pollution – which are not internalized into the decision-making process will cause faulty choices because costs are not appropriately measured. Second, with the future uncertain, as it is when relative and absolute prices change rapidly because of inflation and other manifestations of social and political disorder, it is impossible to formulate an expectation of future prices; long-run decision-making must proceed in an accounting vacuum. Here those trained to think numerically and to maximize profits will seek short-term, measurable advantages, not long-term, unmeasurable ones. Keynes (1936, Ch. 12) recognized this aspect of short-term decision-making.

DECISION-MAKING AND UNCERTAINTY

In a period of uncertainty, the shift in emphasis from long- to short-run profits is characteristic of both industrial and financial institutions. In product markets, American industry attempts to continue using existing production facilities and techniques, not to develop new facilities; to concentrate on product lines in which production processes are understood, not to experiment in the development of new and risky products; and to intensify the sales effort relative to the production effort – not the socially most rational response to economic decline, but reasonable when individual financial salvation is the objective.

It was Keynes (1936, Ch. 12) who recognized that it is uncertainty which prevents the industrialist from attempting to organize the bureaucratic infrastructure necessary to produce and distribute in new and untried ways. Industrialists behave as if the long-term profit rate on new investments and organizations is unknown. Under these circumstances individual industrialists and the bureaucratic organizations with which they are associated are unwilling and unable to forsake profits today for larger but uncertain profits tomorrow.

Uncertainty about the profitability of future production and physical investment is a state of mind, not a state of the world, since the future can never be known. In normal times there is a pretence at firm or probabilistic knowledge about a variety of events including what is relevant for new investment: future price–cost relationships, and the extent of the market. This claim to solidity, this arrogation of future knowledge, is bolstered by numerical calculations of future profitability. There develop scientific predictive arguments in the form of formal mathematical – or less formal literary – models which are often amenable to numerical estimation. Calculation and model-building become a social convention which lends credence to predictions and provides psychological security to those who must make long-run production and physical investment decisions which will decide the financial fate of individuals, corporations and nations. Such confidence is obviously essential if men and women are to proceed.

Moreover, pretending as though one knows the future is not simply an issue of generating motion. To the extent that men and women control their destiny, confidence in the future does, in fact, generate outcomes consistent beyond random occurrence with our estimates of future developments. Indeed, it is the psychological stuff of which an investment boom is made and profits result. Of course, in abnormal times the pretence of firm knowledge about the future is untenable and decision-making is paralysed.

When uncertainty afflicts financial markets and spot prices change rapidly, the slow, patient and steady working of compound interest is replaced by the speculative search for quick profits. Financial investors abandon long-term bonds. The long-term relationship between the interest rate and the 'net productivity of capital' is severed. The long-term interest rate and indeed the prices of other financial instruments which are subject to speculation become social psychological variables subject to the 'hidden forces' which buffet the hopes and fears of financial speculators. As Keynes (1936) often stressed, it is only in normal times that there is a widespread belief that tomorrow will not be too different from today. The recent past provides the conventional basis upon which to judge the future. Prices can deviate only temporarily from this strongly-held view of the normal. Speculators, activated by their concept of normal prices, profit from temporary deviations from normality and by so doing they drive these prices back quickly and efficiently to their normal level or range.

But in abnormal or uncertain times there is no basis for the individual to engage in orderly extrapolation. The stabilizing concept of the normal no longer commands allegiance. Financial survival now requires the speculator to be at or near the head of the herd. The herd instinct, or mass psychology, dominates market behaviour. In this instance, prices are the result of market processes, but these processes are only seemingly based on decentralized decision-making. In unusual times the process is actually subject to a group mind and decentralized units behave as one. The prices of financial instruments, the exchange rate between domestic and foreign currencies, and the prices of other objects of speculation now swing wildly in one direction or another, with speculation intensifying rather than damping the swings.[10]

CONCLUSION

Technology and innovation may be the basis for prosperity. They may provide the means to conserve raw materials. However, there should be no presumption that future expansion implies propelling the United States on the same path that has been followed in the past. Metal working and the automobile need not serve – indeed, probably will not serve – as the driving force behind the next economic expansion. Innovation, coupled with social change may involve the development of new lifestyles rather than facilitate the expansion and extension of old ones.

It is not a matter of efficiency, motivation or ability whether corporate or government bureaucracies, or some combination of the two, decide and implement our technological future. These bureaucracies are not very different in their operational modes. Indeed, in the past many important projects were undertaken on a joint basis. The space programme, Department of Agriculture efforts at plant and animal breeding and raising, and Carter's proposed synfuel project are all examples of the interface between public and private bureaucracies. Indeed, when the society finds it necessary to organize for massive changes, the distinction between private and public loses all meaning.

The issue of how to organize for technological advance and innovation is both an efficiency issue and a political issue. How much regulation and coordinated direction are necessary for the market process to function effectively? Who will choose among the many available options? Who will benefit and who will lose from the choices made? How democratic will the decision-making process be?

Some government coordination is necessary to break the logjam of corporate decision-making. And, in this regard it must be recognized that government bureaucracies are accountable, however imperfectly, to the people through the system of representative government. While the checks and balances of this system reinforce the status quo as parochial interests are defended, the system has proven sufficiently adaptable to facilitate important change. Without regulation – and I use the term in its broad sense to include incomes policies, traditional regulation, and government direction and support for both growing and declining industries – the corporate decision-making process is not constrained by the electoral process. It is accountable only to the market and to corporate boards, private managers, and large stockholders. The hope for America is a compromise between these two parallel decision-making bureaucracies, each accountable to different groups. In addition, in order to be fair and effective, future decision-making must include other groups in society. An incomes programme and an industrial policy are beginnings at such a compromise. The Administration's programme of supply-side economics has been an attempt to eschew compromise and thus it was destined to fail.

ACKNOWLEDGEMENTS

This article is adapted from a paper prepared for the Public Policy Colloquium, University of Notre Dame, South Bend, Indiana, in Gar Alperovitz and Roger Skurski (eds), *New Directions in Public Policy* (Notre Dame Press, spring 1984).

The author wishes to thank Paul Davidson, the editor of *JPKE*, for his many suggestions of both substance and style.

He has also benefited from numerous discussions about the problems of technology and economic growth with Stephen Bennett, Kenneth Flamm, Michael Podgursky, and other members of the Project on Economic Restructuring and the working group on technology and economic growth at the University of Massachusetts, Amherst. Much of his knowledge of the subject of the American corporation comes from his years teaching at the Graduate School of Administration, Carnegie-Mellon University. During these years he was introduced to the view that the modern corporation is best understood as a bureaucratic institution, not as a sole proprietorship.

NOTES

1. Excessive executive compensation – million-dollar parachute clauses in the event of corporate takeovers are a case in point – white-collar crime, creative

accounting, unproductive merger activity and the hard sell of shoddy products, are all instances of social disintegration, not resurrection.

2. There were other problems with the recent version of supply-side economics. The understanding that American society is organized largely (but not exclusively) on the basis of material and not moral incentives provides only an imprecise guide to the formation of economic policy. It does not recommend the size of the differentials necessary to enlist appropriate behaviour. Too large a differential begets ill-will, encourages social conflict, and fosters orgies of conspicuous consumption. Too small a differential discourages effort, blunts initiative and disheartens the ambitious. The proper balance is the difficult goal of national policy.

   Observed differentials vary considerably not only among capitalist societies at a point in time but for a given capitalist society over historical time as well. For example, compared to West Germany and Japan – two very successful capitalist societies – the United States has maintained relatively unequal distributions of income in the post-World War II years, yet each of these three societies would be described as relying heavily on material incentives. And, in the United States the income differentials in the 1920s were much greater than in the 1950s; yet in each instance the underlying incentive system would again be described as a system of material rewards.

   These examples clearly indicate that a capitalist society relies on more than just material incentives to motivate people and that the stakes necessary to organize a system of material rewards can vary considerably. The cultural and historical circumstances of a society are not superimposed on an obdurate human nature dominated by greed and self-interest. Rather, the interaction between individuals and their culture gives rise to an ebb and flow in the importance of material incentives. As the sense of social cohesion weakens – as it undoubtedly did in the United States during the 1970s – monetary rewards admittedly loom large and important. Loyalty, a sense of workmanship, a sense of duty, charitable predisposition, and other non-pecuniary forces determining behaviour were probably weakened as organizing factors during this decade. It does not follow, however, that talented people are unwilling to perform for a modest but secure income. Nor does it follow that the tax cuts of 1981 were accurately targeted toward those who would respond appropriately to the prospect of greater after-tax profits.

3. Ira Magaziner and Robert Reich (1982) have made a statement of the need for market regulation in the American context. The arguments underlying the need for an industrial policy share much in common with the arguments of Paul Davidson (1982), the late Sidney Weintraub (1978), and the late Abba Lerner (1972) in support of an 'incomes programme', broadly construed to mean a programme to establish a politically viable income distribution. For a classic on these matters the reader is referred to the work of Karl Polanyi (1944).

4. Although proponents of this approach are not always sanguine about internal corporate decision-making capability, to date they have not chosen to deal directly with this problem.

5. To be either developed or effectively utilized, new techniques must be embedded in a workplace or in some other social context. This involves the mechanical interface between people and machines as well as interaction among people, the so-called 'human relations' aspect of production. It is in this sense that new investments in machine-embodied innovation go hand in hand with new organizational structures. Thus, changes over time in the

organization of work are no less important than the changes over time in the machine-embodied techniques of production.

6. The national income accounting myth developed that these activities were always productive in some meaningful sense. Certainly some white-collar work is productive. Certainly some service work is productive. But their productivity can be over-stated. Employment (and profits) in these activities was an ingenious social arrangement for distributing the bounty from the goods-producing sector among the people. In a society inclined toward a Protestant work ethic, no other device was likely to have worked to avoid the social disorder and chaos which would inevitably have accompanied 'jobless growth'.

7. The suppression of that individuality steeped in self-indulgence and licence is, of course, not to be bemoaned. Instead, it is that individuality which is the stimulus to creativity and imagination that is the costly loss to the American system. There are many historical precedents for systems that lose their dynamism as creativity gives way to bureaucratic repetition. The great empire of Rome – with highways, theatres, temples, navy and trade, agriculture and manufactures, pre-eminent arms, and successful colonization – decayed and collapsed into the Western darkness. Gibbon, who in accidental irony published the first volume of the *Decline and Fall of the Roman Empire* in 1776, the year Adam Smith published *The Wealth of Nations*, describes this Western tragedy and attributes the Roman failure to internal decay and corruption. Over time 'the minds of men were gradually reduced to the same level, the fire of genius was extinguished, and even the military spirit evaporated.' Blind deference to authority 'precluded every generous attempt to exercise the powers or enlarge the limits of the human mind.' In the end, 'the Roman world was indeed peopled by a race of pygmies when the fierce giants of the north broke in and mended the puny breed' (Gibbon [n.d.], pp. 50, 52).

8. There have been some efforts by large corporations to free themselves from the layers of inflexible managerial control and from the difficulties of providing an adequate incentive system. As traditional approaches to corporate growth have encountered barriers, some corporations have adopted new organizational structures in an effort to develop flexibility and entrepreneurship. Often this requires the spin-off of technical cadres and the development of semi-independent corporate units, the objective being, among other things, to identify and reward individual and small-group contributions and to increase the flexibility of decision-making. However, more common than the internal development of entrepreneurial talent have been efforts to absorb the entrepreneurial skills of smaller firms by purchase or joint venture. It is too soon to determine the success of these organizational efforts.

9. The quantitative vision has certain weaknesses. Too frequently numbers are fetishized and qualitative information and informed judgement are erroneously ignored. There are many examples of numbers blinding the observers. In the 1970s many economic indicators, the Consumer Price Index, census counts, corporate profits and income itself lost their usefulness as inflation made obsolete the index weights, as undocumented migrant flows invalidated the population counts, as inflation and the internationalization of business contaminated estimates of corporate profits, and as the underground economy left much of the national income unreported. Despite this undermining of the statistical intelligence system, economic data continued to be reported and interpreted with sanctimonious reverence.

10. A few instances of unstable market behaviour might prove enlightening. The

price of gold rose from $400 per ounce to $850 per ounce in a three month period in late 1979 and early 1980, and there was a 50 per cent rise in gold prices in a two-month period in the summer of 1982.

Or, turning from gold to common stocks, one might cite as evidence of market instability the two week decline in stock prices in the fall of 1978 when the stock market suffered losses comparable to those inflicted on it by the OPEC oil embargo of 1973, the fall of France in May, 1940, and the collapse of industrial production in 1937–38. In this instance the Dow Jones average fell by almost 110 points, from 900 to 790, while the losses in 'secondary' markets, the American exchange and the over-the-counter exchanges, were larger, with the price of an average share tumbling by 20 and 30 per cent, respectively. We might also note the over 100-point rise in the Dow Jones in the late summer of 1982.

Instability is also in evidence on foreign exchange markets. In the fall of 1978, the dollar fell 14 per cent against the mark and 7 per cent against the yen in a ten-day period. From January to Augsut 1980 the exchange value of the dollar, relative to 15 major currencies, skyrocketed upward from an index value of 95 to a value of 114, only to recede by 9 index points in the following three months.

Lastly, let us note that bond prices and associated interest rates have been remarkably unstable during the 1980–82 period.

REFERENCES

Abernathy, William J. and Hayes, Robert. 'Managing our Way to Economic Decline', *Harvard Business Review*, July/August 1980, **58** (4), 67–77.

Arrow, Kenneth J. *The Limits of Organization* (New York: W.W. Norton, 1974).

Berle, Adolf A. Jr. and Means, Gardner C. *The Modern Corporation and Private Property* (New York: Commerce Clearing House Inc., 1932).

Chandler, Alfred D. *The Visible Hand: The Managerial Revolution in American Business* (Cambridge, Mass: Harvard University Press, 1977).

Davidson, Paul. *International Money and the Real World* (London: Wiley, 1982).

Drucker, Peter F. *Managing in Turbulent Times* (New York: Harper and Row, 1980).

Gibbon, Edward. *The Decline and Fall of the Roman Empire* (New York: Modern Library, [n.d.]).

Keynes, J.M. *The General Theory of Employment, Interest and Money* (London: Macmillan, 1936).

Lerner, Abba P. *Flation* (Baltimore: Pelican, 1972).

Magaziner, Ira C. and Reich, Robert B. *Minding America's Business* (New York: Harcourt Brace, 1982).

Minsky, Hyman P. *John Maynard Keynes* (New York: Columbia University Press, 1975).

Polanyi, Karl. *The Great Transformation* (Boston: Beacon, 1944).

Rapping, L. A. 'The Domestic and International Aspects of Structural Inflation' In J.H. Gapinski and C.E. Rockwood *Essays in Post-Keynesian Inflation* (Cambridge, Mass: Ballinger, 1978).

Simon, Herbert A. Administrative Behaviour (New York: Free Press, 1976).

———. *The New Science of Management Decision*, revised ed (Englewood Cliffs, NJ: Prentice-Hall, 1977).

Taylor, Frederick W. *The Principles of Scientific Management* (New York: Harper and Bros., 1911).

Weintraub, Sidney. *Capitalism's Inflation and Unemployment Crisis* (Reading, Mass: Addison-Wesley, 1978).

Part II
Inflation, Interest Rates and Debt: An International Perspective

Introduction

The essays in this part address such issues as the simultaneous occurrence of slow output growth and high inflation, the so-called stagflation problem, the effect of bank deregulation on financial stability, the causes of high real interest rates, the implications of Third World debt, and the effectiveness of monetary policy in the face of both financial market innovation and the internationalization of financial markets.

Earlier, while at Carnegie–Mellon University, I had studied the stagflation problem with Professor Lucas. We had concluded that the aggregate short-run supply of real output varies with the divergence between actual and expected inflation rates. With high expected inflation rates, output might fall despite rising actual inflation rates.

This explanation met the standards of a scientific theory and it did resolve the stagflation paradox. Although it became a popular accounting for the events of the 1970s, I was uncomfortable with this line of reasoning. I could not accept the notion that exogenous demand shocks along a more or less stable supply curve were responsible for the inflation–unemployment relationship. I thought that the process was more closely related to oil prices hikes, international monetary instability and the export challenge to American industry. These international blows required a restructuring of the American economy and this required stabilization in the large, by which I mean institutional change, not stabilization in the small, by which I mean demand management.

I was unconvinced that the rational expectations assumption resolved my concerns. It seemed to push the rationality assumption too far. After all, the extreme behaviour of unemployment during the deflationary global recession of the early 1980s hardly conforms to a rational expectationist view of the deflationary process.

The four essays in this part emphasize the unfortunate consequences of financial market deregulation. The unstable and unpredictable behaviour of exchange rates, interest rates and stock prices are evidence of the need for more public regulation of national and international financial markets. More importantly, if it is successfully to cope with future and perhaps unavoidable financial crisis, it is important that the authority of the Federal Reserve Bank not be undermined by deregulation mania. This is especially important when the government is disarticulated and unable to manage fiscal policy. These essays argue for a partial reregulation of financial markets. They also contain the view that lower interest rates are the only reliable solution to the international debt problem.

The ideas developed in these essays were presented in lectures at Brandeis University, the Hebrew University in Jerusalem, Florida State University, Middlebury College, the University of California at Berkeley, Davis and Riverside, the University of Nevada at Las Vegas, and Yale University.

5 The Domestic and International Aspects of Structural Inflation *

POLITICAL UNDERLAY OF INFLATION

The American defeat in the Vietnam War, the development of the Soviet SS-9 which ended the American nuclear monopolies, and the breakdown of the Bretton Woods system, which, broadly conceived, defined the monetary, commercial, military and political rules governing the relations among member nations, signalled the end of *Pax Americana*. The disjuncture between the domestic economic and political system organized and predicated on American power and global order, and the reality of declining power and international economic and political incoherence, explain the emergence of stagnation and accompanying inflation in this decade. Moreover, as the American global position wanes, it is increasingly obvious that economic and political events around the world impact on American society in ways previously thought unimaginable. The decline of the dollar, reflecting a loss of confidence in the United States, and the increase in the price of oil, reflecting an inability of the United States to control external events, are perhaps the most salient examples of this unpleasant and destabilizing relationship. The monetary manifestation of these international events is domestic inflation.

The period between the Korean War and the Vietnam War was one of creeping inflation throughout most of the capitalist world. Then came accelerating inflation. While the experience of each country shown in Table 5–1 varies in detail, there is clearly a general

*Reprinted with permission from Gapinski and Rockwood's *Essays in Post-Keynesian Inflation*, Copyright 1979, Ballinger Publishing.

Table 5.1 Inflation rates for selected countries by period[a]

Post-World War II inflation rates (Average annual percentage increase in CPI)			
Country	*1945–48*	*1960–71*	*1971–78*[b]
West Germany		3.3	6.1
France	58.0[c]	4.3	13.2
Italy	57.0	5.0	21.9
UK		4.6	21.3
US	11.3	3.3	9.0
Canada		3.1	11.1
Major oil exporters		(8.0)[d]	(17.0)
Non-oil developing nations		(10.1)	(32.3)

Post-World War I inflation rates (Average annual percentage increase in consumer prices)		
Year	*France*	*Germany*
1914 – 18	138.0	140.0
1919	21.0	223.0
1920	37.7	68.0
1921	– 21.6	144.0
1922	– 1.0	5,470
1923	17.8	75×10^9
1923 – 26	16.9	
1927	– 6.3	

Sources:
a.   Economic Report of the President, 1979; C.S. Maier, 'The Politics of Inflation in the Twentieth Century.' in *The Political Economy of Inflation*, eds. Fred Hirsch and John H. Goldthorpe (1978); and International Monetary Fund and World Bank, *Finance and Development*, 5:2 June 1978.
b.   Computed through the third quarter of 1978.
c.   Retail food prices only.
d.   Figures in parentheses are for the periods 1967–72 and 1974–77.

pattern of accelerating inflation starting in the late 1960s. For the United States, this process was temporarily arrested during the period of wage–price controls, 1971–73, and again during the sharp economic decline in the winter of 1974–75. However, accelerating rates of inflation are clearly in evidence in 1978. One might reasonably suppose that the 1970s are distinctly different from the earlier era. Indeed, except for the inflations associated with the American involvement in World Wars I and II, covering the years 1917–19 and 1941–48, the United States has not, in the twentieth century, experienced so intense an inflation as that of the 1970s.

The creeping inflation of the years 1950 to the middle or late 1960s is usually explained by the relatively high level of employment maintained by means of expansionary monetary and fiscal policies which were implemented under temporarily fortuitous circumstances. The inflationary bias in the system was viewed as resulting from the wage–price-setting process which harboured an inflationary thrust once the threat and reality of mass unemployment faded from memory. Some economists saw creeping inflation replacing mass unemployment as an instrument of 'labour discipline'.[1] This interpretation was too sanguine, since unemployment continued to function in its historic role, albeit in a less extreme form than in earlier decades. The Eisenhower recession of 1957–59 was a kind of muted 'Austrian' remedy for the excesses of the prior expansion. The use of full-scale liquidation and unemployment was unnecessary in the favourable domestic and international environment that existed, and, in any event, might have been politically constrained by the New Deal coalition which at that time had considerable cohesion.

The acceleration of inflation in the late 1960s marked an important structural break in the post World War II era. In my judgement, it is inadequate to explain this acceleration as either the result of adaption to inflation, so that larger doses of it were necessary to maintain employment, or as the result of the changing age–sex composition of the labour force. These explanations assume secular structural cohesion, and are too linear and technical in light of the political and economic events of the 1970s. The institutional conditions which facilitated growth and prosperity in the post-war years were ruptured by the breakdown of the Bretton Woods order.

The collapse of the fragile gold exchange standard in September 1931 and the resulting breakdown of commercial and political relations among the countries integrated by this system of fixed exchange rates, converted a deep depression into the Great Depression.[2] The breakdown of the Bretton Woods system in 1971 has strained and discombobulated nations bound together by this post-World War II dollar standard. The crisis now manifests itself as accelerating inflation, not mass unemployment. The displacement of mass unemployment by inflation is attributable to the principle of the unbalanced budget and willingness to flood the system with credit. While accelerating inflation and high unemployment are undoutedly serious problems, they are not the catastrophe of mass unemployment. Yet the system is fragile, as evidenced by the collapse in industrial production in the winter of 1974–75 and by the stock market and international money market panic in October of 1978. Moreover, the failure of growth has left its trail of wreckage: stagnate real wages, excessive unemployment and excess capacity, urban decay, regional economic disparities, and the usual signs of social disintegration among the weak and the poor.

During the twentieth century, rapid inflations in both Western Europe and the United States have been associated with war or its aftermath. They have occurred when growth has been problematic and when the preconditions for growth have been politically contested. In each case the dynamic issue of growth is intensely intertwined with the immediate problem of distributing a low or slowly growing social product. Thus, not only are the distributional and other institutional preconditions for growth subject to political contention, but the distribution of the existing product is similarly contested. Inflation proceeds so long as there is no political and economic structural resolution to the problem of distribution and growth.

In the present period, not unlike the years after the two World Wars, the preconditions for stability, the *sine qua non* for growth, are only slowly being formulated. Specific problems giving rise to instability include unsettled international commercial and monetary arrangements, the disposition of international and domestic debt, uncertainly arising from the emergence of expensive energy and food, and the distributional conflict emerging from the relocation of industry which requires massive readjustments. In addition, these problems are compounded by the need for higher levels of both public and private investment requiring further containment in the standard of living. These challenges cannot be met under the ground rules which defined the mix of social and private activity after World War II. Logic would suggest the need for extension in economic planning, yet there remains a powerful political thrust to contend with these problems through the workings of an unfettered market. Ultimately, without consensus or without sufficient authority these problems are unresolvable. Under these circumstances, the inflation proceeds, perhaps awaiting some national or international crisis which will force a resolution.

It is in the above sense that continuous inflation is often a reflection of a weak or disoriented government lacking sufficient power to impose solutions. Inflation is never a technical economic problem. The technical details of stabilization policy depend on specific historical circumstances, but the standard list includes tax increases, expenditure cuts, credit restriction, direct or indirect price and wage controls, and the confiscation of excess currency holdings. Recognizing the important political underlay of inflation, it is useful to consider several different visions of the inflationary process which can be expressed in technical terms but each of which has an ideological undertone which is clearly recognized when stabilization problems are considered within the framework of the respective theories.

ECONOMIC THEORIES OF INFLATION

The accelerating rate of inflation following the escalation of the Vietnam War has as its proximate cause both corporate and government deficit spending financed by the expansion of credit. For the government's part, it was the failure to raise taxes, a time-honoured political necessity during war, which was the cause of its contribution to the inflation;[3] for the corporations it was declining profitability coupled with a sustained desire to accumulate physical assets. In summary, for the period 1965 to 1969 the inflation was a result of classic 'demand-pull' pressures. It is for the next nine years that the reasons for continuing inflation are less obvious.

A view common enough among economists of the monetarist persuasion is that the accelerating inflation during the 1970s results from adaptive inflationary expectations coupled with the insistence on the part of state authorities to maintain too low an unemployment rate. For monetarists, larger and larger doses of monetary injection are necessary to maintain employment, although eventually this process is viewed as self-defeating in the sense that employment no longer responds to inflation. Explosive inflation is the price of commitment to high employment. If one accepts all of the necessary assumptions, accelerating inflation and rising unemployment in the 1970s are consistent with this theory. However, it would seem that excessive monetary expansion is at best a proximate cause of inflation. Why is it that such monetary expansion occurs? For some monetarists it is simply 'error', or 'bad economics', which accounts for the behaviour of the state. For others it is a defect in the democratic process defined in a narrow electoral sense. Vote-maximizing governments accede to the pressures from potential beneficiaries of inflation.

There are several difficulties with the monetarist view.[4] It is assumed that the stock of narrowly defined money is supply-determined; that changes in this stock determine changes in effective demand; and that changes in effective demand impact on prices, not quantities. There is nothing obvious about any of these three assumptions. However, even if these assumptions are accepted, one is also required to adopt a Walrasian vision of the underlying economic process, for the theory proceeds to analyse the impact of price changes on production and employment under the assumption of atomistic competition. The view that market participants engage in neat and orderly calculations might have some appeal in periods of international prosperity and peace – perhaps it was appropriate for the years 1870 to 1913 when Britain dominated the world's economic scene or for the years 1950 to the middle or late 1960s, when the United States imbued the capitalist world with order and growth. In such periods, market participants might have some basis upon which to contemplate, formulate and extrapolate in response to current market events. When the underlying process is stable and knowable, they may have some basis upon which to 'see' the future. But this is hardly the situation in the 1970s. Modern economies are deeply embedded in a global financial and commercial system. Wars, revolutions, mass starvation, racial and nationalistic conflict, global political realignments, or the breakdown of imperial systems, have no special importance in this Walrasian vision, except perhaps to alter the exchange rate. More likely, in the conflict-ridden world of the 1970s, uncertainty abounds. Determinate, well-specified models of future price developments simply do not exist. No one, not even the CIA, could have predicted recent Iranian events which are currently impacting on prices.

There are other problems with the monetarist view. The central bank does not control credit; it simply controls the elements in its balance sheet. Rapid financial innovations during the late 1960s and throughout the 1970s have created financial markets in which the central bank has only loose and imperfect influence. The development and expansion of Eurocurrency markets, commercial paper markets, commercial bank liability management, and trade credit in its numerous forms have created a loose and uncertain relationship between changes in the composition of the central bank's balance sheet and the volume of credit. In the present financial environment, the central bank can 'pull on a string', but only at the risk of breaking it.

Finally, central bank decision-making does not come directly under the influence of the electoral process. The decision-making apparatus of this institution is dominated by bankers and large industrialists. Unless one is to argue that, like Mr Dooley's Supreme Court, the central bankers follow election returns, the voters have no way of coercing these men. Moreover, the democratic process is more complex than that implied by a narrow electoral vision. Admittedly, the electoral process plays a role in influencing policy but so does group 'pressure politics'. Graft, corruption, ideology, strikes and street demonstrations are all in evidence in western democracies. Witness the striking gains of the civil rights movement in the 1960s which were based on marches, demonstrations and general political pressure. Or consider the current struggle over nuclear power. It is not limited to the electoral process. Finally, the narrow electoral view cannot explain the failure of the Eisenhower administration to stimulate the economy in 1960. While the electoral trade cycle model contains an important insight concerning the role of elections, it remains far too incomplete.

Opposed to the Walrasian view is a bewildering variety of theories all of which parade under the banner of 'price-wage' equations. These theories have in common the assumption that effective demand determines quantities, not prices. These quantities discipline the wage and price-setting process. If unemployment and excess capacity are increased sufficiently, wage and price increases are attenuated. Once quantities are set, money wages are determined by power relations in the labour market. Prices are set by a mark-up pricing equation with product market power establishing the mark-up. In this approach, money and credit are seen as endogenous and elastic, partly because of the institutional characteristics of the credit markets and partly because of political considerations which guide the monetary authorities.[5] Borrowing from natural rate theorists, adaptive inflationary expectations are recognized, and as individuals, unions and corporations adjust to the experience of inflation the inflationary process becomes self-generating.

The approach which sees inflation as the monetary manifestation of a wage–price process requires an explanation of why inflation is intense in some periods, as in the 1970s, and modest in others, as in the years from 1950 to 1965. What causes shifts in either the wage or price equation? A variety of explanations have been offered, most of which stress the notion of union 'wage-push' rather than monopoly 'price-push', probably because of a belief that despite widespread mergers and conglomeration, the degree of product market power has not significantly increased in the past fifteen years.[6] These explanations differ widely in their emphases but all seem to stress the unacceptability of existing income differences and the resulting distributional dissent. There are theories of 'new consciousness' and 'frustration' and more complex theories of ongoing sociopolitical structural processes that undermine the necessary status or hierarchical ordering of capitalist society.[7] While these arguments and theories provide important insights into the workings of capitalist economies, they do not address the transition from creeping inflation to rapid inflation. After all, the sociopolitical forces at work have been operative for well over a hundred years. Why do they now manifest themselves as rapid inflation? Moreover, any theory of the underlying structural causes of inflation must account for the occurrence of rapid inflation and slowly growing product.

Far more promising is the idea that accelerating inflation is rooted in the concept of an 'aspirations gap'. When the rise in the living standard is halted by the failure of growth or a deterioration in the terms of trade (defined here as the total quantity of exports necessary to acquire a given quantity of imports), it is assumed that if real demands are maintained, an 'inflationary gap' arises. As individuals, unions and corporations attempt to maintain their standard of living and their real profits (or their growth rates), they lay claim, through the price-wage-setting process, to a larger share of the declining (or less rapidly rising) social product. The result is inflation.

In broad terms, something akin to this may have occurred in the industrialized capitalist world during the decade starting in the late 1960s. The terms of trade deteriorated and growth in output slowed. Table 5.2 shows the growth rates in real Gross National Product for the years 1960–78. Clearly there has been a slowdown in recent years. According to the aspirations view, whatever explains this slowdown explains the accelerating inflation.

Table 5.2 Annual percentage growth in real GNP for several countries, 1960–1978

Country	1960-73 (Average)	1974-78 (Average)
US	3.9	2.3
Japan	10.5	3.7
West Germany	4.8	1.7
France	5.7	2.8
UK	3.2	1.0
Canada	5.4	3.4
Italy	5.2	1.9

Source: Economic Report of the President (1978), p. 139.

The poor performance of real wages and profits are consistent with the idea that distributional strife has intensified in the 1970s. Despite the rather impressive performance of profits in the past year, a variety of statistics measuring the profitability of the capital stock indicate that profits, like real wages, have performed poorly in the 1970s as compared to earlier years.[8] This is indicated, for example, by the rate of return on depreciable assets for nonfinancial corporations which averaged 10.7 per cent between 1970 and 1978 as compared to 13.0 per cent over the period 1955 to 1970.[9] This reflects the slow growth rates in real output in the 1970s as compared to the earlier decade.

In the United States this slowdown in growth is seen in the failure of real wages to grow at their traditional rate. Between 1950 and 1965 real wages as measured by average hourly earnings, grew at the rate of 2.6 per cent per annum, while in the period 1966–78 they grew at only 0.8 per cent per annum. If we measure real wages in terms of real take-home pay, they have not grown in over a decade.[10]

We may view the issue in terms of a different statistic. A short-term decline in either the level or rate of increase in real per capita consumption will not in general intensify conflict. Rather, what is required is a long-term or permanent decline in this measure. When this occurs, antagonisms are heightened and workers at all levels of the wage hierarchy struggle to maintain their living standards. For the United States, the statistics on real per capita consumption indicate that the rate of growth in the 1970s has fallen short of its 1960s performance. In the earlier decade this statistic grew at the rate of about 5 per cent per annum. In the latter decade it grew at a rate of only about 3 per cent per annum. However, this comparison belies the true decline in the standard of living during the 1970s for the average American.

The population figures on which this statistic is based do not include illegal aliens who have been entering this country at what may well have been an accelerating rate since the early 1970s when economic conditions deteriorated in many parts of Latin America, from whence the great majority have come. To this factor should be added the point that since the advent of high inflation rates there has been a marked deterioration in the quality of many commodities. Henry Ford's Pintos and good old Harvey Firestone's radials are the more deadly examples of this phenomenon. But in less flagrant ways, plastics, polyesters and other chemicals invade and degrade almost every aspect of American consumption. These phenomena result from cost-cutting efforts throughout American industry and although they are not easily accounted for in the price index, it is plausible to conclude that measured price statistics understate the rate of inflation. Consequently, the rate of growth in real per capita consumption is overstated for the 1970s, perhaps by a very wide margin.

There are two other reasons why the data on real consumption growth in this decade overstate the improvement in the standard of living. Between 1974 and 1975 there occurred a rather sharp and unexpected increase in the female labour force participation rates. As a result, part of the subsequent improvement in consumption has been achieved through an increase in the number of multiple worker families. Finally, a not insignificant part of the growth in real consumption after the spring of 1975 has been financed by instalment credit rather than from current income or past savings.

Increased distributional conflict, which manifests itself as rising wages and prices, will necessitate the expansion of credit in order to finance a higher level of nominal income. In recent years endogenous credit has served to finance even higher levels of income. Moreover, in inflationary times speculative fever rises. Changing relative prices in existing assets like land, real estate, jewellery, and many other items which are the traditional objects of speculation excite and tempt those in quest of a fast buck. Speculation is often credit-financed as the banks see an opportunity to make large profits in their role as speculative brokers. The credits granted by banks, once used in a speculative venture, may find their way into the more normal channels of trade. In this way, speculation in existing assets will alter the demand for newly produced commodities. But this is not the only channel whereby speculation in existing assets can influence the price and wage structure. Increased land prices, as well as that part of the increase in interest rates associated with the speculative demand for credit, will be incorporated into the general price of housing and foodstuffs. Whether this incorporation is quantitatively significant remains a matter of conjecture.

Within the price–wage vision of the inflationary process, then, we have a situation in which money wages, prices, and credit are all expanding apace. The price–wage process, however initiated, has self-generating properties, for once the process is in motion, inflationary expectations undoubtedly take hold and propel prices upward. During the 1970s this process has been continuously refuelled by the deteriorating terms of trade and slow growth. In turn, both the terms of trade and the growth rate have been impaired by international instability and the decline in American hegemony.

THE DECLINE IN THE DOLLAR

The dollar declined about 25 per cent on a trade weighted basis between 1970 and 1978. This decline increased the domestic price of

internationally-traded commodities, including agricultural products. From 1970 to 1978, US agricultural exports rose from \$7.2
billion to \$28.0 billion, an event that undoubtedly raised domestic
food prices. During the same period, the increased dollar price of oil
has raised the price of all oil-based products and has significantly
contributed to the increased cost of oil imports. In 1970, the dollar
value of oil imports was \$3.1 billion; in 1978, over \$40 billion. Both
the decline in the dollar and the OPEC price increases are rooted in
the decline of American hegemony. This is obvious in the case of oil,
but I would also ascribe dollar depreciation to the weakening of
confidence in the United States as a military, political and economic
power. This loss of confidence has impacted on the dollar, primarily
through short-term capital flows reflecting an unwillingness to hold
dollar-denominated assets as a store of value.[11]

While the relative price increases in food and energy have been
large (see Table 5.3) these externally caused shocks by themselves
cannot account for the inflation of the 1970s.[12] But a rise in the price
of internationally-traded commodities can affect domestic prices by
altering wage and price decisions which impact on domestically
traded commodities.

Table 5.3 *Percentage growth rates of food, energy and other prices, 1971–78*

Period	Food Prices	Energy Prices	Prices of All Items Less Food and Energy
	%	%	%
II/71-IV/72	3.9	3.7	3.1
IV/72-I/74	19.6	22.3	4.6
I/74-III/75	8.8	13.9	9.7
III/75-II/78	6.2	6.9	6.6
IV/77-IV/78	11.3	7.0	8.6

Sources: Economic Report of the President, 1979, and *St. Louis Federal Reserve Review*
(December 1978).

It is best to study the effects of deteriorating terms of trade in real
rather than price terms. A decline in the terms of trade will, like a
slowdown in the growth rate, generate price inflation to the extent
that the deterioration is quantitatively significant and that it impacts on workers and corporations who attempt to defend their
standard of living and maintain their profits. Between 1970 and

1978, United States import prices (in dollars) rose by 30 per cent relative to US export prices, which means that the US had to export 30 per cent more commodities or attain foreign credits in order to finance a given quantity of imports. In 1978, the United States imported $170 billion in merchandise which required $51 billion more per year in exports or in trade credits than in 1967 ($234 per person or $396 per family of four per year).[13] Deteriorating terms of trade have impacted significantly on the American standard of living.

DOMESTIC INVESTMENT AND INTERNATIONAL INSTABILITY

There are other less obvious but important inflationary effects of international instability and declining US power. Domestic investment, along with global investment, may have been contained by increasing international instability and uncertainty. Investment both creates effective demand and increases effective supply. For any given growth rate of the labour force, the higher the level of net investment, the higher the growth rate in labour productivity. Weakness in investment relative to labour force growth may partially account for the poor performance in labour productivity in this decade. It can also partially account for the slow growth rates in output since 1973.

The breakdown of the Bretton Woods system and the emergence by default of floating exchange rates, increased trade restrictions, and currency controls have fundamentally altered the basic institutional environment in which world-wide investment occurs.[14] Perhaps more than anything else, the 1970s is a period of uncertainty with respect to the international flow of financial capital and commodities. In the absence of reasonable predictability concerning the world-wide distribution of production, flow of commodities and movement of financial resources, it is difficult for multinational or indeed even national corporations to embark on long-range investment projects anywhere in the world. In short, the recent efforts at competitive devaluations, exchange controls and import restrictions, as well as the heightened conflict of developed and developing nations and oil-producing and consuming nations, not only affect the level of international trade but provide a partial but significant explanation of the failure of investment in the capitalist world economy to recover vigorously from its low point in 1975.

The problem of evaluating the impact of uncertainty on

investment is certainly not a new one. It was widely discussed in the 1930s. One of Keynes' major theoretical contributions was to stress the potential importance of uncertainty on the investment decision. In the *General Theory*[15] he said:

The state of long-term expectation, upon which our decisions are based, does not solely depend...on the most probable forecast we can make. It also depends on the confidence with which we can make this forecast—on how highly we rate the likelihood of our best forecast turning out quite wrong. If we expect large changes but are very uncertain as to what precise form these changes will take, then our confidence will be weak.

The state of confidence, as they term it, is a matter to which practical men always pay the closest and most anxious attention. But economists have not analyzed it in general terms. In particular it has not been made clear that its relevance to economic problems comes in through its important influence on the schedule of the marginal efficiency of capital...*The state of confidence...is one of the major factors determining the...investment demand-schedule.* (Emphases added.)

Keynes is arguing that a perceived potential for large changes in the environment for which no firmly held probabilities can be attached is the essence of a weak 'state of confidence'. And the 'state of confidence' is one of the main determinants of investment demand. To Keynes the impact of risk and uncertainty was the problem of the 1930s. Both his theory of liquidity preference and of the marginal efficiency of investment dealt with the problem of risk and uncertainty and their relation to investment and, ultimately, employment and growth. Although there are striking differences between the 1930s and the 1970s, the impact of uncertainty on investment is one of the major problems of both eras. It may be an important explanation for slowly growing productivity both in the United States and abroad.

INTERNAL AND EXTERNAL STABILIZATION

The term stabilization has both a narrow and a broad interpretation. When the underlying structure of both the domestic and international economy is stable and ordered, in the sense that the potential for profitable growth exists, stabilization means simply demand management, sometimes combined with minor institutional adjustments required to facilitate growth following stabilization. Perhaps this is best exemplified by the Eisenhower stabilization effort in the late 1950s; or, going further back in time, one can cite the stabilization policies in France in the mid-1920s, when a sound bourgeois government under Poincare replaced a left coalition. In the latter instance, a 15 per cent per year inflation (see Table 5.1) was suddenly halted by the technical device of a mild tax increase and more importantly by the restoration of confidence. In both instances stabilization was achieved in the framework of relatively stable international conditions and, in a broader sense, domestic and international conditions conducive to growth. There was no need significantly to alter the proportion of income devoted to investment, no need to re-establish workplace productivity, no need to alter real wages, no need to reconstruct international financial and commercial order, and no need to adjust to a significant alteration in the relative prices of the two major sources of energy – food, and oil.

Both the Walrasian and the 'price-wage' visions of the inflationary process are in a strict sense concerned with stabilization in the narrow usage of this term. Within the pure logic of these theories, any reduction in nominal spending, however caused, will moderate the inflationary thrust of the system.[16] The price of this reduction is unemployment and excess capacity. However, the theories are too general and the world is too complex to permit anything other than the qualitative judgement that declining demand will necessitate additional unemployment. There is, however, a strong presumption present in the Walrasian view that when the stabilization effort by the state is definitive and credible, the resulting unemployment will not be too severe.[17] On the other hand, within the 'price-wage' vision there is the presumption that those forces generating an inflationary thrust in the system will be resistant to the disciplinary impact of unemployment and excess capacity.[18] The necessary level and duration of disciplinary unemployment could be so high and so long as to create a political and economic crisis far deeper and less predictable in its impact than the inflationary crisis itself.

In retrospect it is now clear that throughout the 1970s, demand restraint never represented a real anti-inflationary option, although I would not express this position in terms of the deterioration in the trade-off between inflation and unemployment (i.e. a shifting Phillips curve). This vehicle of expression implies a stability and predictability in the underlying process that simply does not exist. It seems preferable simply to assert that the financial process and the production–employment process are too unstable to contemplate demand restraint as a means to reverse the inflationary thrust of the system.

Since the middle of the 1960s, financial and production processes have become increasingly resistant to anti-inflationary demand management. In the 'fragile' financial sector, 'near panics' occurred in the 'crunch' of 1966, in the 'second crunch' of 1971, and in 1974–75, when OPEC price increases and foreign exchange speculation caused the collapse of the Herstatt and Franklin National Banks.[19] The intense drive in October 1978 to unload both ownership claims in American industry and the dollar revealed the continued underlying instability of the financial system.

The fragility of the financial process is paralleled by the unsoundness of the production–employment process. Four years ago when a Republican administration attempted an orderly retrenchment of the economy by means of monetary and fiscal restraint, industrial production collapsed and unemployment rose to its highest level since the 1930s. They quickly retraced their steps. Taxes were cut and money was thrown at the economy. With the help of monetary ease and a $60 billion deficit, depression was avoided both here and abroad.[20] The economy is no less vulnerable to rapid descent now than it was in 1974–75. So long as there remains uncertainty concerning such matters as the relative price of energy, the parameters of the international system, the limits of state activity, and the distribution of income, the economy will exhibit instability and unpredictability.

The inflation is an alternative to a worse outcome, mass unemployment. The inflation unfolds under the impetus of the distributional struggle over wages, prices, and taxes and the process of national and international restructuring proceed under the inflationary umbrella.[21] When or if the preconditions for growth are established and when there is sufficient power to impose an explicit parliamentary or authoritarian distributional solution through tax, credit and state expenditure policy, stabilization will follow. But stabilization will fail unless there is a resolution to issues relating to real wages, authority at the workplace, parliamentary incoherence and international disorder. Stabilization in the broad sense of the term involves the internal settlement of relations among the numerous levels of workers and between capital and labour generally. It involves also the external settlement of relations among national interests. In a general sense, stabilization in the large means institutional change, not demand management. Keynes himself was aware of this distinction. Discouraged by the experience of ending mass unemployment in the 1930s, except in the case of Nazi Germany, he wrote in 1940[22] 'It appears to be politically impossible for a capitalistic democracy to organize expenditure on a scale necessary to make the grand experiment which would prove my case, except in war conditions.'

STABILIZATION AFTER THE TWO WORLD WARS

Inflation associated with slow growth or abnormally low output is containable when the preconditions for rapid growth are re-established. This structural interpretation of inflation is consistent with the experience after World Wars I and II, when rapid inflations were ended by a combination of domestic and international reconstruction. Internationally, the re-establishment of order entailed agreements to contain the use of certain competitive tactics, especially devaluation, quotas, and tariffs. The objects were to create order and predictability within the framework of an integrated world economy. These agreements were embodied in rules which restrained nationalistic policies. These rules were defined by the gold exchange system, which was partially erected by 1926, and later by the Bretton Woods system, which was well established by the early 1950s.

The achievement of the fragile international order after World War I, and the more durable order after World War II, facilitated and were facilitated by domestic stabilization. In the most general terms, domestic stabilization required a resolution concerning the mix of collective and private activities and the role of labour organizations in the workplace and in the parliamentary system. The resolution of these issues defined the ideological and distributional preconditions for growth. After both wars, domestic inflation proceeded at extremely high rates, both in Western Europe and the United States, until these issues were resolved in either conflict or compromise. In the post-World War II years, resolution came under the auspices of the social democratic compromise which entailed a significant role for both the state and the unions. This is to be distinguished from the post-World War I solution in which labour organizations were either severely contained – as in the cases of Germany and Great Britain – or excluded from the mass production industries as in the cases of the United States and France.[23]

CONCLUSIONS

The stabilization of prices requires the restructuring of both the domestic and international economy. Restructuring is required to create the conditions necessary for economic growth, an absolute prerequisite for calming distributional strife. At the international level, government restructuring is presently predicated on large military expenditures and a continuation of the American internationalist thrust, defined within a system of freely moving commodities and financial capital. The alternative, American retrenchment within the context of a smaller dollar bloc, a lower level of military expenditures, restrictions on the movement of commodities as well as direct and financial investment, has not been widely articulated. However, there is no logical reason to base stabilization on the concept of internationalization. Free trade and economic growth are by no means necessary partners.

Domestically, restructuring seems to be moving in the direction of an earlier, bygone era. This is seen in the efforts to extend market relations and to reduce collective activity. These efforts include the call for deregulation, a reduction in the social wage, the elimination or attenuation of health and safety standards, the push for right-to-work laws and the support for other antiunion legislation, tax reductions, and a variety of other proposals to extend market relations. The alternative, of course, is to extend the role of the government in democratic planning for energy, health, food, credit allocation and a host of other areas. Planning entails the logical extension of the macro-planning system of the post World War II years and it is only within the framework of a broader system of planning that wage and price controls are workable. The challenge is how to blend the unique American experience into a democratic planning system. The danger, of course, is the emergence of planning in the service of a selected few.

The issue, it seems, is whether the United States will move to the political right or left. The inflation has increased ideological and political tensions that have long been suppressed by economic growth. Economists who are unwilling to take the broad view will be unqualified to deal with these problems.

NOTES

1. Martin Bronfenbrenner provides this interpretation in his essay, 'Some Neglected Implications of Secular Inflation', in *Post Keynesian Economics*, ed. K.K. Kurihara (New Brunswick, NJ: Rutgers University Press, 1954).
2. Charles Kindleberger develops this interpretation in his book *The World in Depression, 1929-1939* (University of California Press, 1973). The argument traces back to William A. Brown, Jr, *The International Gold Standard Reinterpreted, 1914-1934*, Vol. I (National Bureau of Economic Research, Inc., 1940).
3. The choice of wartime inflation as in World War I, or of price controls followed by postwar inflation as in World War II, as opposed to tax increases during the

war, represents the substitution of a distributionally uncertain inflation tax burden for a distributionally certain income and corporate tax burden.

4. In a previous incarnation, I found monetarist theories compelling. Age and experience have altered my perceptions of the world.

5. The issues raised by the Walrasian versus the wage–price visions of the inflationary process hark back to an old controversy in Anglo-Saxon economics between the Currency School represented by Ricardo, and the Banking School, represented by Tooke. One wonders how much the science of economics has progressed since the Napoleonic Wars.

6. Within the framework of the wage-price view of the inflationary process, many economists ascribe causal primacy to the excessive money wage demands of organized workers. Price increases are primarily a reflection of these union excesses. The inflationary process unfolds on the basis of the numbers trade union leaders pluck from the air. This stress on union wage policy rather than the corporate determined mark-up is a curiosity most charitably explained by theoretical inconsistency. By accepting a determinate theory of corporate pricing behaviour – the theory of continuous profit-maximization – economists eschew a monopoly theory of inflation unless the extent of monopoly significantly increases prior to or during an inflationary episode. But, by similar reasoning, one would eschew a union theory of inflation if it were assumed that unions, like monopoly corporations, attempted to maximize an objective function containing the single argument, total economic rents. This would freeze union power, but admittedly at considerable cost in terms of realism. I would judge that unions sometimes sacrifice rents for employment gains while at other times rents per worker rather than total rents might be of primary concern. But by similar reasoning profit-maximization might not be appropriate under all circumstances either. As argued by Herbert Simon (*Administrave Behavior*, New York, The Free Press, 1976), corporations are complex political and social units seeking numerous goals which can only tautologically be expressed as profit-maximization. Were corporations to shift from, say, share-maximization to profit-maximization, the level or rate of increase in product market prices would increase. In this event, increased mark-ups would precede wage increases. Of course, as a practical matter wages and prices rise together during inflationary episodes. None the less, it is only the willingness of many economists to accept corporate profit-maximization while at the same time holding no firm theoretical position on union wage policy that biases them toward a 'wage-push' rather than a 'price-pull' theory of inflation.

7. An excellent exposition of these ideas can be found in Fred Hirsch, *Social Limits to Growth* (Cambridge, Mass: Harvard University Press, 1976). See also John H. Goldthorpe, 'The Current Inflation: Towards a Sociological Account', in *The Political Economy of Inflation*, eds. Fred Hirsch and John H. Goldthorpe (Oxford, Martin Robertson, 1978).

8. The cyclical upswing beginning in the spring of 1975 has, as usual, contributed to an improvement in profitability. Moreover, in 1978 the rapid increase in prices might well have benefited capital as opposed to labour in the distributional struggle. It should also be added that data on average profitability belie the performance of profits in many industries. In particular, the profits of energy companies have performed comfortably since the OPEC price increase in the fall of 1973.

9. See *Economic Report of the President* (1979), p. 128. While the measurement

of profitability is notoriously inaccurate, especially in inflationary periods, other measures of profitability such as cash flow as a per cent of GNP indicate profit problems in the 1970s.

10. Of course, measured real family consumption has grown during this period, but that is because of an increase in multiple workers and consumer instalment credit, especially after 1975.

11. I recognize that domestic inflation has some impact on the exchange value of the dollar, but I wish to stress that it is incorrect to assume that the willingness to hold a particular currency as a store of value depends only on its expected purchasing power in terms of commodities of the country of issue. Among other things, in periods of uncertainty, asset holders have no basis upon which to formulate price expectations. Moreover, in unsettled times it is unclear what the future rules of convertibility will be. After all, there are historical examples of nations which have blocked foreign holdings of domestic currency. Great Britain after World War II prevented exports by blocking the sterling holdings of Commonwealth nations. In general, it is difficult to predict the resolution to the problem of the dollar overhang, an issue which has been elevated to primary concern in the 1970s.

12. Presumably using a model with fixed coefficients in consumption and production, the Council of Economic Advisers estimates that a 10 per cent devaluation of the dollar 'will generally result in a roughly 1.5 per cent increase in prices by the end of a 2- to 3-year period...' (*Economic Report of the President*, 1979, p. 43).

13. In 1978 the United States was in deficit on commodity account, and the excess of imports over exports was financed by foreign central banks which were accumulating short-term treasury paper. In effect, the United States continues to act as though the dollar is still the reserve currency. For an interesting discussion of this behaviour, see E. Ray Canterbery, 'The International Monetary Crisis and the Delayed Peg', *Challenge* (Nov./Dec. 1978).

14. This section is based on a study jointly conducted with Professor James Crotty.

15. John M. Keynes, *The General Theory of Employment, Interest, and Money* (New York: Harcourt, Brace and World, 1936), pp. 148-9.

16. The level of government expenditures has by itself no sacrosanct impact on the rate of inflation. If the government is pursuing an anti-inflationary policy, it can just as effectively impact on the inflation by raising taxes as opposed to cutting relief spending. Indeed, there is no technical reason why a reduction in spending must be achieved through the government sector. Consumer instalment credit, which permits some workers to deficit finance, or business credits which permit some corporations to deficit finance, are no less candidates for budget balancing than the federal government, if the sole objective is to moderate inflationary pressure. Indeed, the government sector, including both the federal and state sectors, has at the present time a balanced budget with the federal deficit roughtly offset by state government surpluses. Were it not for matching grants and other federal transfers to the state governments, it would be the states rather than the federal budget which would be in deficit. The political conflict revolving around state and federal budgets – as seen in Proposition 13 pathology is best understood as reflecting distributional strife and it is only peripherally related to the problem of terminating the current inflation.

17. There is, of course, a difficult problem in specifying what constitutes a credible programme and this raises issues of stabilization in the large.

18. At no point in the post-World War II era has recession failed to moderate advancing prices. The issue is not whether recession is deflationary, but rather its cost in terms of employment and overall political and social stability, both here and abroad.
19. The best treatment of the financial fragility hypothesis is found in Hyman Minsky's *John Maynard Keynes* (New York: Columbia University Press, 1975).
20 I use the term depression rather than recession in the sense in which the term was used in the pre-World War II period. The term recession is of post-World War II coinage and has meaning only in the context of effective Keynesian-style stabilization policies. I take it as obvious that under current circumstances no one seriously proposes fine-tuning the economy. I also presume that the reader is sensitive to the economic and political distinctions between the term depression and the events of the 1930s, the Great Depression. The latter term should be reserved to identify a global event in which the commercial, financial and political institutions of capitalism are wrenched from their moorings.
21. The distributional outcome of inflation is uncertain because the process is blind and arbitrary. It is the simultaneous underlying restructuring that is the significant distributional process during an inflationary episode. Thus, the distributional effect of inflation is best studied after its conclusion. This does not deny the fact that some groups benefit (at the expense of others) from inflation per se, but these distributional effects will vary from one inflationary experience to another. Although the distributional effects of the current inflation are difficult to identify because tax evasion has significantly increased in the past decade, I have little doubt that a redistribution from low to high income groups has occurred. For an insightful discussion of this and related issues, see Bernard Malamud, 'Keynes and the German Inflation' (unpublished, University of Nevada, Las Vegas).
22. John M. Keynes, 'The United States and the Keynes Plan', *New Republic* 103 (29 July 1940): 158.
23. In Germany, the return to the ten-hour workday in late 1923 signified the loss of parliamentary power by the Social Democratic party and its union allies. It signified also the demise in the authority of the factory councils. In both France and the United States, organized labour was excluded from any significant role in the mass production industries by their resounding losses in the strikes of 1919 and 1920, and by the depression of 1920–22. In the case of France, their strike defeats and the depression of 1920 '...effectively subdued proletarian militancy for a decade and a half'. (C. Maier, *Recasting Bourgeois Europe*, Princeton, NJ: Princeton University Press, 1978: 158). For the United States, the events of 1919–22 ushered in the heyday of the open shop movement, labour injunctions, anti-trust laws applied to labour, the American Plan, and Taylorization.

6 The Causes of High Real Interest Rates in the 1980s*

INTRODUCTION

The theory and practice of interest rate determination is a subject of passionate concern to the borrower, the banker, the rentier and the politician. Over centuries of recorded history, the subject has created profound political controversy. It is not surprising that the interest rate is sometimes controlled, often regulated and always watched. In recent years the interest rate or, more precisely, the complex of interest rates, has been at an average level unprecedented in both Europe and the United States since the beginnings of the Industrial Revolution. This development demands an explanation and in this essay we suggest the reasons for the present unfortunate predicament. The analysis requires that we discuss both history and theory.

Our explanation will stress the decade-long process of financial market deregulation – a process activated by the decline in political authority – coupled with the obsession to gamble and speculate in financial assets – an obsession given opportunity for expression by economic stagnation which shifts entrepreneurial attention from producing new things to acquiring existing things.

While we offer a unique explanation for the causal relationship between deregulation and high interest rates we do not claim originality for the allegation. Albert Wojnilower, Henry Kaufman and others have warned of the dangers in deregulating the banking industry. Wojilower argues that during periods of monetary

---

*Written with Stephen J. Bennett, and revised in the summer of 1983.

113

restraint, regulated interest rate differentials encouraged disintermediation and a contraction of the construction industry.
Deregulation eliminates this highly sensitive transmission mechanism. Without the leverage of disintermediation, monetary
restraint will contain spending only after very substantial interest
rate increases. In a similar vein, Kaufman contends that unregulated
competition gives rise to 'spread banking' – borrowing short and
lending short – an institutional development which allegedly raises
the interest rate on bank deposits and bank loans.

For a proper perspective on this issue, one should keep in mind
that high interest rates cannot account for the global economic
decline of the 1980s although they did exacerbate matters. High
rates certainly weakened the demand for housing and autos,
intensified the repayment problems of consumers, corporations and
Third World borrowers, increased federal deficits, contributed to an
already very unequal distribution of income, and burdened the
society by the recreation of a rentier class. However, over-capacity,
high oil prices, international monetary disorder, the breakdown of
domestic and international political authority and changing military
relationships defined the broader context in which interest rates
operated.

FROM FINANCIAL CRISIS TO REGULATION

The Napoleonic financial retreat of the early 1930s, followed by the
unpleasant disclosures of the Pecora Hearings and preceded by
several decades in which the Progressives advocated regulation,
stimulated an effort to reconstitute the integrity of the banking
system by legislatively strengthening the process of bank regulation.
In both the 1933 Glass–Steagall Act and the 1935 Banking Act, as
well as in the 1933 and 1934 Securities Acts, an effective regulatory
process was enacted. These regulatory efforts were designed to
instill depositors with confidence – a goal achieved by inspection,
supervision and deposit insurance as well as by the creation of an
effective public authority capable of acting as a lender-of-last-
resort. They were designed to prevent destructive financial market
competition – a goal achieved by containing through balkanization
and forced segmentation the powerful market drive to merge,
branch, consolidate and to otherwise grow and expand. And they
were designed to facilitate the control of credit by enhancing the
effectiveness of 'monetary policy' – a goal achieved by granting the
Federal Reserve Bank the power to regulate interest rates

(Regulation Q powers) and more effectively to control bank reserves.

THE DEREGULATION OF INTEREST RATES

The financial regulatory system established in the 1930s served the nation well during the twenty-five years of global prosperity after World War II. It was a sound foundation for the construction of an orderly and regulated global financial system. But by the early 1970s a reverse process of international and domestic financial market deregulation was in motion, and we are now witnessing the concluding phase of this process. The supply of credit and the interest rate have been largely deregulated. The quantity of credit and its price are now determined by the market, not the Fed. As John Garrett has so persuasively argued, the Fed and the private financial market actors have always been involved in a game-theoretic struggle, the outcome of which depends not only on the mechanical tools available to the Fed and its monetary targets – its instruments and its objectives – but on its authority and power as perceived by finanical market participants. In a period in which *de facto* and *de jure* deregulation of domestic and international financial markets is the dominant theme of American economic policy – the current 'non-system' of gyrating exchange rates and the Financial Deregulation Act 1980 being important cases in point – it should not be surprising that the markets, not the Fed, dominate the movement of both interest rates and the quantity of credit. Naturally, there are many who have expressed concern over these developments. For example, Henry Kaufman says, 'the passion to regulate has now been replaced by the passion to deregulate.' He argues for a balanced approach to the financial system. He warns that if carried to excess, deregulation will undermine the ability of the Fed to maintain the fiduciary responsibilities of financial institutions.

Excessive deregulation creates a paradoxical financial situation. Consider, for example, bank loans to Argentina, Brazil, Mexico and other Third World borrowers. The terms and size of these loans are determined by unregulated global market forces but the difficulty of repayment becomes a public issue when non-performance threatens confidence in the global banking system. Under these circumstances, public authority must secure the safety of bank deposits, maintain the international flow of credit, and assist in maintaining confidence in the global banking system.

Indeed, the banks demanded public assistance and were willing to accept *limited* regulation. However, over a decade of financial market deregulation has weakened the ability of the Fed to meet its responsibilities in this instance and made more difficult the problem of maintaining confidence during the silver market crisis of 1980 and during the Penn Square affair of 1982.

THE DECISION OF OCTOBER 1979

In the early years of the 1970s, powerful market forces were undermining the effectiveness of the monetary authorities to regulate both the exchange rate and the interest rate. In the spring of 1973 the monetary authorities surrendered on the issue of exchange rates and the stage was set for a speculative assault on the dollar. There eventually occurred a sawtooth dance of dollar depreciation choreographed by speculators and rooted not in market fundamentals or 'essentials' – that is, changes in domestic and foreign internal prices, incomes, credit supplies, and interest rates – but in the actions of speculators speculating on what they think other spectators think.

In the late autumn of 1978 an unsuccessful effort was made to arrest the senseless depreciation of the dollar. Supported by the Bundesbank, the Fed borrowed foreign currencies and attempted to outmanoeuvre the banks and other speculators. They failed. The dollar continued to decline. The exchange rate could not be regulated. A year later, prompted by the fall in the dollar, the Fed moved significantly toward the final decontrol of interest rates, a decision coming less than six years after the decontrol of exchange rates and, we remind the reader, only a little over a year after the second decontrol of oil prices.

In October of 1979, the Federal Reserve announced a change in operating procedures. They would target bank reserves, not interest rates. In the pre-October regime, the Federal Reserve targeted the federal funds rate and fixed this rate in the very short-run within narrow limits by buying or selling US securities. In the post-October regime, the Federal Reserve targeted nonborrowed reserves and again attempted to meet its target by open market operations.

This action should be interpreted in its proper historical context. Interest rates were rising for well over a year prior to the October decision. Moreover, in the decade before the October decision, legal ceilings on interest rates were being relaxed or removed on a piecemeal basis. A partial list of relevant events will highlight this point: in June of 1970 Regulation Q ceilings on large time deposits with 30 – 89 day maturities were suspended; in May of 1973 ceilings were removed on large time deposits with maturities exceeding 90 days; in January 1974 NOW accounts were authorized in some states; in early 1974 came the rapid spread of unregulated money market mutual funds; in April 1975 banks were authorized to liberalize transfer restrictions from savings accounts to demand deposits; in June, 1978 six-month money market certificates were introduced by banks; in July 1979 a floating ceiling for time deposits with a maturity of over four years was introduced. The October decision is best viewed as a logical continuation of this process of decontrol, not as a voluntary shift in monetary policy in the usual sense.

Finally, following the October decision, Congress continued the decontrol process by passing the Deregulation Act in March 1980 which, among other things, mandated the phased removal of all ceilings on interest rates still subject to Regulation Q rulings. The process of interest rate deregulation was being completed.

In the three years following the October 1979 decision, the level and variability of interest rates rose to historically unprecedented highs, inflation subsided and a protracted global economic contraction developed. This sequence of events raises two separate issues. First, is the Fed responsible in some meaningful sense for the rise in interest rates? Secondly, is the rise in interest rates an important explanation for the emergence of global, large-scale unemployment? We concentrate on the former question.

A WEAKENING FED

The October decision by the Fed is frequently described as a purposeful policy embarked on by an independent and self-confident central bank. In point of fact, the Fed was severely constrained in its ability to influence events. In the game-theoretic struggle between the Fed – a powerful regulator when armed with the legislation and political mood of the 1930s but only a semblance of its former self by the late 1970s – and the actors in financial markets – a hesitant and cautious crowd in the decades following their panicky financial retreat in the early 1930s but now undisciplined and free wheeling in their quest for financial gain – the Fed has been outmanoeuvred as global military and political events have undermined market-regulating authority both at home and abroad.

Recall that the central bank has been unable to prevent private banks from wildcatting abroad, unable to supervise or monitor loans to Third World borrowers, unable to regulate the emerging competition among commercial banks, thrift institutions and investment banks, unable to prevent defection from the Federal Reserve System, unable to control the innovation of new credit forms, unable to reliably influence the creation of checkable deposits, unable to depend on a disarticulated Congress, and unable to coordinate its policies with those of other central banks despite the development of financial markets dominated by the international flow of money. The rise in interest rates and the behaviour of credit aggregates is certainly worthy of a more promising culprit than the Federal Reserve Bank.

ALTERNATIVE VIEWS OF THE INTEREST RATE

If we abandon the idea that the monetary authorities control the interest rate, then we are challenged to explain why current interest rates are so high. We propose that abnormally high interest rates, not unlike abnormally low or high exchange rates, result from portfolio or asset adjustments in response to deregulation and speculation. For the sake of completeness, however, we shall also discuss the loanable funds explanation for high interest rates which stresses restrictions on the monetary base and government deficits; and the Fisher–Friedman explanation which stresses inflationary expectations.

DEREGULATION, SPECULATION AND HIGH INTEREST RATES

As is well know, Keynes separated the rate of interest from the rate of profit and made the rate of interest a result of a portfolio choice between bonds and money. In this approach the current interest rate depends among other things on the market's expectation of the future rate of interest. This approach permits valuation to involve an element of arbitrariness, due largely to uncertainty about the future.

Under normal circumstances the market will form what Keynes called a *conventional* view of what the rate of interest would be – based largely on the evidence of the recent past. If interest rates have fluctuated within a certain range the market will expect that they will continue to do so. As long as the conventional view prevails, the rate of interest cannot fluctuate very much, since speculators then act as stabilizers.

While *stabilizing* speculation maintains a conventional rate of interest, we must be alert to the other possibility: *destabilizing* speculation driving the price of assets far outside their normal or conventional range, leading to the breakdown of the convention and thus to beliefs in the market that the unwarranted and unexpected price movement will continue. Such beliefs, if widely held, will upset asset prices even more, and in the process will destroy all semblance of conventionality and normality in the market. Recent experience can be interpreted in these terms.

A full year before the October decision, long-term interest rates were drifting upwards after having been bounded in the 6–7 per cent range for almost eight years. Interest rate stability was a result of the Fed's policy coupled with the market's belief that rate stability would continue. The Fed's October announcement caused an earthquake in bond markets. It drove some speculators out of the market entirely, and converted the more adventurous to destabilizing bears. The long rate rose even higher as a result. Bulls who believed that the demand for output as a whole was elastic to the rate of interest were grievously punished for their error of interpretation and timing, leaving the market completely to the bears. Any semblance of the old-established normality of the bond market vanished.

This explanation contains a number of shortcomings. As a simplified schematism the basic Keynesian approach employed here is elegant and insightful, but it classifies assets into the two categories, money and bonds, not into real assets and money assets, a classification more relevant for today. Moreover, the actual or expected changes in the value of money will affect asset preferences, and this consideration must be explicitly recognized to analyse the more complex world of the 1970s and 1980s.

As far as changes in the value of money are concerned, money and debts are on a par with each other, since both are denominated in money terms. People fearing inflation will not flee from holding debts to money, unless they also fear for the creditworthiness of the debtors whose paper they are holding.

For the purpose of analysing the response of asset prices to the prospect of inflation, the dividing-line must be fixed between those assets whose returns (and therefore whose prices) are fixed in money terms, i.e. cash, bills, bonds, and those which are not, i.e. equities and real goods. A certain prospect of inflation will raise the values of the latter and depress the values of the former, but only within limits. The limits are due to the fact that many sorts of real goods, especially capital equipment, are only imperfectly liquid. People will prefer to get a hedge against inflation by going into those assets, such as equities and commodities, which are relatively liquid due to the fact that they are continuously traded on organized markets.

Given current circumstances, it is more relevant to recast these ideas in terms of speculating (gambling) rather than hedging (insurance). When uncertainty prevails, the concepts 'prospect of inflation' or 'expectation of inflation' have only a vague meaning. In this circumstance it is the actual rather than the expected inflation that influences the interest rate.

The social conventions governing the distribution of income and wealth erode during inflationary episodes and distributional conflict results. Under these circumstances, relative prices change and economic growth is slow or problematic. These propositions are roughly consistent with the American and European experiences in the years immediately after World Wars I and II and in the years after the first oil price shock in the autumn of 1973. With the combination of conflict, rapidly changing relative prices, and slow growth, speculation abounds. The rich must protect established wealth. The acquisitive newcomer must attempt to seize it. The gambling spirit infects the markets for real estate, equities, collectibles, gold and foreign exchange to name the more prominent speculative vehicles of recent years. The prices of speculative assets can change quite dramatically for speculators are driven by mob psychology. In these circumstances, the rising returns on speculative assets force an increase in interest rates so long as they are decontrolled.

The reader should be reminded of just how virulent speculation has been since the mid-1970s. Witness, for example, the dramatic rise in the German mark in the 1970s, the meteoric ascent of the dollar in the 1980s, the incredible increase in gold prices at several intervals in the 1970s and early months of 1980, the unfortunate explosion in real estate values in cities like Washington, DC and Los Angeles in the 1970s, and the curious climb in equity values during the past year.

For the purpose of analysing the effect of interest rate decontrols, the dividing-line is now fixed between those assets whose returns were regulated – bills, bonds and deposits – and those assets in which returns were unregulated – gold, foreign exchange, equities, real estate and collectibles. The self-generating increase in the price of speculative assets will be reflected in the market for assets fixed in money terms – 'bonds' and interest-bearing money – as interest rates on these assets are 'pulled-up'. Of course, were the banking system to accommodate these speculative ventures with new credit the rise in the interest rate might be slowed. Decontrolling the interest rate in the face of intense speculation is a recipe for rapidly rising interest rates.

While the above argument offers an explanation of the rise in interest rates in the last four years, it is less potent in explaining why interest rates have remained so high. It is possible that the conventional range of the long rate has moved to a permanently high level. Of course, when the market's view of a conventional price changes, it does not do so without reason. Among the reasons often cited for the continuation of high rates are the rapid rise in the US money stock since mid-1982, the current and prospective large government deficits, and fears of a domestic recovery that will revive the private demand for credit. If the markets believe that one or all of these factors cause interest rates to be high, then in fact they do have such an effect. Fears that rates will be high in the future cause them to be high today – and the longer this situation persists, the more likely it is that a new convention will be established.

Loanable Funds: Another Explanation of High Interest Rates
The most widely-held alternative to the portfolio or asset-preference explanation for high interest rates, in which prices move in order to equilibrate the demand for a stock of assets to the available supply, is an approach in terms of the supply and demand of credit or loanable funds, both treated as flows per unit time. In this approach the demand for credit depends on prices and the scale of output, while the supply of credit depends on the voluntary savings of the public and on the amount of new credit-creation by the banking system. In this view, lending is a supply of finance which is demanded in order to undertake some productive process and what is demanded and supplied in the money market is savings which will be used to further productive investment, both measured as flows.

However, because asset preferences change for many reasons (of which the demand and supply of finance is only one) the portfolio approach seems more appropriate in abnormal circumstances when asset preferences often change abruptly. In the portfolio approach it is the general state of asset preferences which determine the rate of interest at which funds will be supplied for finance, and not the conditions of demand and supply of finance which determine the rate of interest.

Despite abnormal circumstances, the loanable funds framework has a powerful appeal in recent efforts to explain high interest rates.

A view common enough on Wall Street and in Washington is that after October 1979, the Fed successfully contained the growth in the monetary base and the credit superstructure assembled on this base. With a highly inelastic demand for credit, the restriction of credit supply caused only a small decline in the rate of credit growth but an extraordinarily large increase in interest rates. Credit demand was interest-insensitive because borrowers both at home and abroad were confident that the Fed would fulfill its lender-of-last-resort commitments. Moreover, the largest borrower, the US government, knew it could pay interest and principal by issuing additional debt when taxes were difficult to collect. In this view, government deficits – indeed, corporate, consumer and Third World deficits as well – contribute to high interest rates.

This explanation has weaknesses. There is no reliable empirical relationship between government deficits and the interest rate. Moreover, the view that a combination of credit supply restriction and inelastic credit demand accounts for the high interest rates in the 1980s conveniently ignores over a decade of financial innovation which has rendered the multiplier relationship between the monetary base and the supply of credit problematic. Credit is endogenous.

Expected Inflation: Another Explanation for High Interest Rates
Another common explanation for high interest rates is that expected inflation affects the present by raising the nominal rate of interest. For those who are enamoured with long-run theories of competitive equilibrium, the interest rate is a result of technology interacting with culture and *expected* inflation rates, all of which determine the investment and savings decisions of a society. Savings decisions result from the choice between present and future consumption while investment decisions are based on expected profitability. The expectation of inflation influences current savings and investment decisions and raises the nominal interest rate in proportion to the expectation of inflation. In other words, both savers and investors reason in real, not nominal terms.

While the above considerations are of interest, in this matter it is experience not theory which dominates the popular imagination. High interest rates and current inflation are statistically associated, at least in some rough way. However, the recent rise in the inflation corrected interest rate, from an average value of 3-month T-bills of about 2 per cent in the 1970s to over 5 per cent in the 1980s indicates considerable sluggishness of interest rates when inflation rates decelerate.

We are not very comfortable with the resolution of the recent paradoxical relationship between current inflation and nominal interest rates by the argument that the nominal interest rate impounds the *expected* inflation rate rather than the actual inflation rate. According to this line of argument, the *expected* inflation rate remains high despite a slowdown in the *actual* inflation rate and as a result, the nominal interest rate remains high. Recall, however, that the expected inflation rate is not observed. It is a cloudy concept, especially in periods of uncertainty.

Equilibrium reasoning has its limitations. In periods disrupted by unsettling political and military events, social conventions are unglued and disequilibrium prevails. Under these circumstances, behaviour is not reliably predicted from models which imply order and meticulous calculation and the nominal interest rate can deviate significantly, and for long duration, from its value as determined by the interaction of savings and investment. This was the situation in the interwar years and it is the situation again today.

CONCLUSIONS

Walter Bagehot, the nineteenth-century editor of the *Economist* and commentator on central banking, asserted that 'Money will not manage itself...' However, during most of the nineteenth century, Americans did not manage their money, although with the formation of the Federal Reserve system in the early part of this century, the United States began a serious, long-term effort to correct this failure. Unfortunately, this effort is now being relaxed and monetary policy is losing its effectiveness.

There are no lack of proposals for arresting the process of deregulation. Recently, Chairman Volcker has called for a temporary moratorium on financial market deregulation. Henry Kaufman and others have proposed some reregulation of financial markets including the extension of reserve requirements on money market funds, the regulation of bank lines of credit and an increase in the Fed's authority over margin requirements. In a different vein, Henry Reuss has proposed a more democratic process for choosing Open Market Committee members, and a consolidation of regulatory activities including consideration of a unified federal regulator over banks and other financial institutions. At this stage, however, the specifics of reregulation are less important than re-establishing the principle that regulation is an appropriate and desirable approach to managing the nations' credit supply.

We may conclude by placing the discussion of monetary policy and its effects in the present context, which is one of combined inflation and stagnation. In the last fifteen years, growth of nominal income and output has been more and more growth of prices, and less and less (sometimes not at all) growth of real output or employment. In recent years the economic system has contained rising prices, or, if you please, preserved the value of money, but in avoiding the Scylla of permanent inflation, the system sails perilously close to the Charybdis of world depression. The dilemma is obviously a real one.

There have been some who have denied the dilemma. Inflation, they claim, is everywhere and always a monetary phenomenon, in the sense that rising prices, whatever their origin, can always be restrained or eliminated by a sufficiently tight monetary policy which refuses to validate the price increases. However current evidence indicates that in the short run – and the short run has now persisted for three years – the weight of adjustment falls on output and employment as much as prices. This is in accordance with Keynes' doctrine. Monetarist optimism that the world might work in another fashion has been dashed by experience. But the disappointment of facile hopes has not yet led to theoretical debate. Wall Street and Washington continue to half-believe in an unsatisfactory theory for want of anything better: and as long as their belief continues its ghostly existence the threat of world depression is not over. Indeed, we may have already reached the point where purely financial expedients of any sort will be insufficient to revive consumption and investment in the face of world-wide overcapacity and lack of confidence.

At the time of writing (July 1983) we seem to be in a situation where a rate of interest which, to the surprise of many economists, turned out to be low enough to revive the housing and consumer durable industries in the US (at least temporarily), is at the same time far too high to ease the cash flow problems of Europe and the Third World. Even more worrisome is the fact that interest rates have recently been drifting up from already punitive levels.

The theory that high interest rates caused the current global crisis is unsatisfactory. We reject the notion that the Fed exogenously raised interest rates which in turn impacted on real output. Instead, we view the interest rate as an endogenous variable reflecting excessive speculation and economic disorder, not causing it. Any useful explanation of the global economic decline of this decade cannot ignore the decline in political authority, the first and second oil price shocks, the increase in manufacturing capacity in Japan and in the Third World, the breakdown of international financial and commerial order, and the change in military technology. Unfortunately, there is no simple mechanical explanation for the recent events nor, indeed, for the equally profound events of the early 1930s. Simple explanations build cadres, not understanding.

America is politically disarticulated and those who insist on the superiority of unregulated market processes are motivated by either self-interest, ideological blindness, or the recognition that without consensus we have no choice but to pursue a 'do nothing' or 'wait and pray' policy. Unfortunately, however, in financially and militarily unstable times, the unregulated financial market is itself unstable. Until a democratic consensus for financial market regulation can be formed, we must live with the constant threat of market disintegration.

7 Speculation, Deregulation, and the Interest Rate*

Interest rates during the 1980s have been at average levels unprecedented in both Europe and the United States since the beginnings of the Industrial Revolution. For those who believe that the Fed controls the interest rate, these high rates are attributed to the October 1979 decision to target bank reserves rather than interest rates. In this view, the Fed succeeded in its effort to indirectly regulate the interest rate by restricting bank reserves, and hence credit. However, because financial innovation (for example, NOW and money market accounts) has greatly weakened the link between reserves and credit, we reject this view. We propose instead that the abnormally high interest rates resulted from portfolio or asset adjustments in response to interest rate deregulation (the October 1979 decision as well as the decontrol of interest rates on deposits) coupled with generalized speculation in asset markets. This explanation will be empirically contrasted with the loanable funds explanation which stresses the flow supply and demand for credit and the Fisher–Friedman explanation which stresses inflationary expectations.

THE THEORY

When severed from the rate of profit, the rate of interest is sometimes viewed as resulting from a portfolio choice between bonds and money.[1] Under these circumstances, the interest rate will

---

*Written with Lawrence B. Pulley, and first published in *The American Economic Review*, vol. 75, no. 2, May 1985.

depend among other things on the market's expectation of the future rate of interest. Of course, uncertainty about the future imparts an unavoidable element of arbitrariness in determining the interest rate. However, under normal circumstances the market will form a conventional view of what the rate of interest will be – based largely on evidence from the recent past. As long as the conventional view prevails, speculators act to stabilize the market. However, when the normal structure is disrupted, destabilizing speculation can drive the prices of assets far outside their conventional range, leading to the breakdown of the convention and to expectations that the unwarranted price movement will continue.

Between 1969 and 1977 the long-term rate of interest on Treasury bonds fluctuated between 6 and 7 per cent – due to the Fed's policy of pegging interest rates as much as to the market's belief that such a policy would continue. For eight years the convention held and stabilizing speculators were appropriately rewarded for their activities. But in 1978 the long rate started to drift up, and a year later the Fed renounced the policy pegging interest rates. Some speculators, whose stabilizing activity had been based on the Fed's policy of targeting interest rates, were driven out of the market entirely. However, because it was understood that the Fed's abandonment of interest rate targets and the continued decontrol of deposit rates were signalling higher interest rates and a recession, many others were converted to destabilizing bears. The long rate both rose and became unstable.

Although this simple Keynesian approach is insightful, classification of assets into the two categories, money and bonds, fails to illuminate the effects of decontrol. For the purpose of analysing the decontrol of interest rates, the dividing-line must be fixed between those assets whose returns were regulated (bills, bonds and deposits) and those assets in which returns are uncontrolled (gold, foreign exchange, equities, real estate and real goods).

Rapping (1979) has argued that a form of destabilizing speculation (i.e. seeking short-term profits by betting on self-sustained asset price changes and disregarding fundamentals) and generalized inflation are common in periods in which the social conventions governing the distribution of income and wealth erode and distributional conflict results. Under these circumstances, relative prices change and economic growth is slow and problematic. With the combination of conflict, rapidly changing relative prices, and slow growth, speculation abounds. The gambling spirit infects the markets for real estate, equities, collectibles, gold and foreign exchange to name the more prominent speculative vehicles of recent years.

The expectation (if not always the reality) of very high returns now dominates behaviour. Under these circumstances, the regulation of interest rates will prevent the self-generating increase in the prices of speculative assets from raising the interest rate. However, once interest rates are deregulated, the return on interest-bearing assets will rise in accordance with the high returns expected on speculative assets. Depending on attitudes towards risk, the interest rate might not equal the anticipated yield on the speculative assets.

We refer to the explanation of high interest rates described above as the portfolio or asset-preference explanation, in which prices move in order to equilibrate the demand for a stock of assets to the available supply. The most widely-held alternative view is based on the flow supply and demand of credit or loanable funds. In this approach, the demand for credit depends on prices and the scale of output, while the supply of credit depends on the voluntary savings of the public and on the amount of new credit creation by the banking system.

A third explanation for high interest rates is that the prospect of inflation or expected inflation affects the present by raising the current nominal rate of interest. In this long-run competitive equilibrium view, the interest rate is a result of technology interacting with culture and expected inflation rates, all of which determine the investment and savings decisions of a society. Savings decisions result from the choice between present and future consumption while investment decisions are based on expected profitability. The expectation of inflation will be impounded in current savings and investment decisions in such a way as to raise the nominal interest rate in proportion to the expectation of inflation.

METHODOLOGY AND RESULTS

The Model
In expectations form, the basic Fisher equation relating the nominal interest rate, R, expectations of the real rate, r, and expectations of the inflation rate, π, can be written

$$(1) \qquad R_t = E_m(r_r|\phi_{t-1}) + E_m(\pi_t|\phi_{t-1}),$$

where ϕ_{t-1} represents the relevant information set available at the beginning of period t and E_m represents market expectations. Assuming the distribution of $E_m(r_t|\phi_{t-1})$ to be centred on a constant long-run equilibrium rate, ρ, with short-term fluctuations given by u_t, (1) becomes

$$(2) \qquad R_t = \rho + E_m(\pi_t/\phi_{t-1}) + u_t.$$

The earliest attempts empirically to examine Fisher interest neutrality have focused on (2) above, regressing nominal interest rates on actual or lagged inflation rates or some measure of expected inflation. The results have not been satisfactory. Coefficients on expected inflation are often significantly less than the predicted value of one, and vary across both time-periods and maturities.

In response to mounting evidence that the expected real rate itself is not constant, recent studies have allowed changes in the real rate to be associated with changes in a number of other variables (often in the context of general equilibrium macroeconomic models). John Carlson (1977a) and Vito Tanzi (1980) examine the effects of changes in real activity or business cycle behaviour (i.e. shifts in the *IS* curve). In downturns, for example, the (expected) real return to capital falls. If, as a consequence, the demand for loanable funds falls more than the supply, the (expected) real interest rate falls. Of course, if shifts in the *IS* curve can affect real rates, so should shifts in the *LM* curve. James Wilcox (1983) and others have included money supply growth as a proxy for the well-known liquidity effect. Some have suggested increased money growth volatility as an explanation of high rates, but David Berson (1983) argues that interest rate volatility is the more important volatility measure, particularly given the role of risk premiums in the finance literature.

In this paper we employ the augmented Fisher relationship to examine the hypothesis presented in the introduction and detailed above. The model we adopt is the following:

$$(3) \qquad R_t = E_m(r_t|\phi_{t-1}) + \beta_1 E_m(\pi_t|\phi_{t-1}) + u_t,$$

$$(4)\ E_m(r_t|\phi_{t-1}) = \rho - \beta_2 E_m(\pi_t|\phi_{t-1})$$

$$- \beta_3 LIQ_t + \beta_4 ACT_t + \beta_5 \sigma_{Rt} + v_t,$$

where $E_m(\pi_t|\phi_{t-1})$ is included among the explanatory variables in (4) to allow incomplete adjustment to the level of expected inflation. *LIQ* is a liquidity variable reflecting shifts in the *LM* curve. *ACT* is a real activity variable for shifts in the *IS* curve, and σ_{Rt} is a measure of interest rate volatility to incorporate changes in the risk premium. ρ is the constant component of the expected real rate. All beta coefficients are expected to be positive. β_1 is not constrained to unity to allow for tax effects. Combining (3) and (4) yields

$$(5) \qquad R_t = p + \beta_0 E_m(\pi_t | \phi_{t-1}) - \beta_3 LIQ_t$$
$$+ \beta_4 ACT_t + \beta_5 \sigma_{Rt} + w_t,$$

where $\beta_0 = \beta_1 - \beta_2$ and $w_t = u_t + v_t$. With a suitable proxy for $E_m(\pi_t | \phi_{t-1})$ (5) can be estimated with ordinary least squares.[2]

We now relate the model described above to the explanations of high interest rates previously discussed. Expression (3) is the simple inflationary expectations model. The liquidity and real activity variables in (4) capture the effects of the Keynesian money-bonds asset choice and changes in the demand for loanable funds. Interest rate volatility is included to control for risk. In Part C below, we present evidence that the inflationary expectations and loanable funds models do not explain interest rates after October 1979. Furthermore, the reported significance of a naive shift variable is consistent with the presence of increased speculative activity.

The Data

The expected inflation series is based on the Livingston surveys computed by the method described in Carlson (1977a, b). The survey represents an average of predictions by economists of the value of the *CPI* six months from the survey months of June and December. Therefore, the nominal interest rates used in this study are the six-month treasury bill rates prevailing in those months. The period consists of the fifty observations 1959:6 through 1983:12.

The liquidity variable (*LIQ*) is measured as the growth rate in seasonally adjusted and revised *M*1 (current dollars) over the most recent quarter. For example, the value corresponding to the June observation is the growth rate implied by the first- and second-quarter observations on *M*1. The measure of real activity used is the growth rate in real *GNP* over the last six months (two quarters).[3] A measure of interest rate volatility, σ_{Rt}, is computed as the standard deviation of monthly observations on three-month Treasury bill rates over the most recent twelve-month period.[4]

Results

To examine the hypothesis described above, we construct the model in (5) above with a duplicate set of explanatory variables (including the constant) which take on the value of zero through 1979:6. With these changes the estimating equation becomes

$$(6) \qquad R_t = (\rho + \rho') + (\beta_0 + \beta_0') \, E_m(\pi_t | \phi_{t-1})$$
$$- (\beta_3 + \beta_3')\mathrm{LIQ}_t + (\beta_4 + \beta_4') \, ACT_t$$
$$+ (\beta_5 + \beta_5') \, \sigma_{Rt} + w_t,$$

where the primed values represent changes in the coefficients after October 1979. A positive and significant value of $\hat{\rho}'$ would be consistent with our hypothesis that after October 1979, traditional economic relationships in interest rate determination were replaced by what we have labelled speculative factors. These influences helped keep interest rates abnormally high. (Unfortunately, this test is not very powerful since a positive $\hat{\rho}'$ could result from some other omitted variable or influence.)

Table 7.1 presents the results of estimating various versions of (6) above using an iterative maximum-likelihood procedure to correct for first-order serial correlation. Credit controls were in effect during the first half of 1980. Therefore, a dummy variable taking the value one for 1980:6 was included to avoid any distortions introduced by these controls. All variables with the exception of expected inflation were reduced by their sample means. The constant terms can therefore (roughly) be viewed as the real rate when inflationary expectations are zero and *LIQ, ACT*, and σ take on their sample mean values.

Column 1 of Table 7.1 gives estimates of the basic Fisher relationship. The estimates in column 2 are from the model in (5) when coefficients are not allowed to adjust in the post-1979 period. The model in column 3 differs from that in column 2 by the inclusion of a dummy variable for the post-1979 period. Column 4 contains estimates for the full model in (6).

Consider the results in Table 6.1. The unprimed values are consistent with our expectations and with the results of other studies. The one notable exception is the statistically insignificant coefficient on the real activity variable.[5] There is also some evidence of coefficient adjustments after 1979. The adjustment on the *LIQ* variable coefficient ($\hat{\beta}_3'$) indicates a possible increase in the importance of the liquidity effect. This lends some support to the conclusion of Richard Clarida and Benjamin Friedman (1984) regarding the contribution of slow money growth to the recent high rates. The negative coefficient adjustment on expected inflation ($\hat{\beta}_0'$) is consistent with the view that interest rates have continued to rise (or remain high) in the post-1979 period despite declines in actual and expected inflation. Therefore, it may not be reasonable to posit lagging inflationary expectations as a reason for the high rates.

Table 7.1 Interest rate regressions semiannual: June 1959–December 1983

Independent variable	Specification			
	(1)	(2)	(3)	(4)
Constant				
$\hat{\rho}$	2.88[a]	3.33[a]	3.04[a]	2.93[a]
	(3.56)	(3.91)	(5.73)	(4.95)
$\hat{\rho}'$	–	–	2.06[a]	5.89[a]
			(2.64)	(3.04)
$E_m(\pi_t\mid Q_{t-1})$				
$\hat{\beta}_0$	.88[a]	.78[a]	.73[a]	.76[a]
	(6.00)	(5.34)	(6.17)	(5.84)
$\hat{\beta}_0'$	–	–	–	– .53[a]
				(– 2.19)
LIQ				
$\hat{\beta}_3$	–	– .19[a]	– .16[a]	– .13[a]
		(– 4.07)	(– 3.20)	(– 2.22)
$\hat{\beta}_3'$	–	–	–	– .24[a]
				(– 2.04)
ACT				
$\hat{\beta}_4$	–	.026	.007	.010
		(.61)	(.16)	(.20)
$\hat{\beta}_4'$	–	–	–	.11
				(.92)
σ_R				
$\hat{\beta}_5$	–	.30[a]	.28[a]	.42
		(2.09)	(1.93)	(1.01)
$\hat{\beta}_5'$	–	–	–	.23
				(.48)
Dummy (June, 1980)				
$\hat{D}$	– 6.35[a]	– 8.52[a]	– 8.26[a]	– 9.91[a]
	(– 7.75)	(– 9.28)	(– 8.36)	(– 7.17)
R^{2b}	.88	.91	.91	.92
SSE^c	49.2	35.8	33.9	28.5
$D\text{-}W^d$	2.20	2.16	2.02	1.88
$AR1^e$	.76[a]	.81[a]	.61[a]	.62[a]
	(8.38)	(9.88)	(5.30)	(5.14)

Note: 50 observations; *t*-statistics are shown in parentheses.
[a]Significantly different from zero at the .05 level (one-tailed test).
[b]R^2 adjusted for degrees of freedom.
[c]Sum of squared errors.
[d]Durbin-Watson statistic.
[e]Iterative *ML* estimates of the first-order serial correlation coefficient.

One potentially troublesome aspect of the results in Table 7.1 is the large and statistically significant first-order serial correlation coefficient (prior to correction). Although some serial correlation is often present in analyses over time, such large values could indicate the omission of an important variable from the analysis of the post-1979 period. Of course, the dummy variable included for the period is at best an imperfect proxy for the factors we described on p. 127. Furthermore, the residual serial correlation is not a product of the post-1979 period alone. When expression (5) is estimated for the period 1959:6 through 1979:6, the computed serial correlation coefficient is .70.

There is evidence in Table 6.1 for our assertion that a substantial component of the increase in interest rates since October 1979 cannot be explained by the model in (5), even when all slope coefficients are allowed to adjust. The coefficient $\hat{\rho}'$ is positive and statistically significant. Furthermore, the average of the last nine residuals (observations 1979:12 – 1983:12) for the model in column 4 is .06. If $\hat{\rho}'$ is constrained to be zero and the model in column 4 is re-estimated, the average of the last nine residuals becomes .48. (Based on the residual standard deviations, the standard deviations of both these averages is approximately .25.)

CONCLUSIONS

Recent high interest rates are not explained by factors which appear in traditional interest rate models. Similar results have been found in the study of foreign exchange markets where neither the purchasing power parity flow approach nor the interest differential asset approach can account for the behaviour of the dollar after 1977. Some have attributed the high value of the dollar to speculative behaviour in which decision making is contaminated by a crowd psychology. We contend that while direct speculation in assets fixed in money terms may account for high interest rates, the high rates may also be attributed to generalized speculative activity throughout the economy which pulled interest rates up once they were decontrolled.

Of course, our empirical evidence is only suggestive. With the usual caveats of caution, we conclude that unless speculation is penalized or otherwise deterred, continued deregulation of interest rates could mean continued high interest rates. The excessive speculation of the 1920s was penalized in the bath of red ink caused by the financial market panic of 1929–33. In the 1980s, on the other hand, the Fed has wisely renounced this dangerous medicine for financial overexuberance. Unlike the earlier period, it has actively played its role as a lender-of-last-resort. Of necessity, selective penalties are now needed and the authority to administer them will require some relaxation in the process of financial market deregulation.

NOTES

1. The discussion in this section draws selectively on an unpublished paper by Rapping and Stephen Bennett (1983).
2. Of course, no available measure of $E_m(\pi_t|\phi_{t-1})$ can be expected to be error-free so an errors-in-variables problem exists. However, as Tanzi has shown, the coefficients do not seem to be particularly sensitive to the use of the Livingston survey data and *OLS* or any of several instruments and *2SLS*. Since the Livingston data will be used in this study, we note the finding of Kajal Lahiri and Mark Zaporowski (1984) that the Livingston data consistently underpredict true expectations, in which case coefficients based on the Livingston data are over-stated.
3. In this model, federal tax and spending behaviour influence the interest rate by their impact on economic activity. This by no means exhausts the avenues whereby the deficits might affect the interest rate. In particular, deficits could alter interest rate expectations and asset pricing behaviour.
4. The three-month rates were used rather than the six-month rates because the monthly observations on these rates were more readily available. The Livingston survey data are from the Federal Reserve Bank of Philadelphia. The interest rate and money supply data are from the Federal Reserve. The *GNP* figures are from the Department of Commerce.
5. As an additional proxy for real activity, the ratio of employment to non-institutional population was used. The measure is employed by Carlson (1977a), but produced results no different from those in Table 6.1.

REFERENCES

Berson, David W. 'Money Growth Volatility, Uncertainty, and High Interest Rates', *Economic Review, Federal Reserve Bank of Kansas City*, November 1983, 23-38.

Carlson, John A. 1977a 'Short-Term Interest Rates as Predictors of Inflation: Comment,' *American Economic Review*, June 1977, **67**, 469-75.

———, (1977b) 'A Study of Price Forecasts', *Annuals of Economic and Social Measurement*, Winter 1977, **6**, 27-56.

Clarida, Richard H. and Friedman, Benjamin M. 'The Behavior of U.S. Short-Term Interest Rates Since October, 1979,' *Journal of Finance*, July 1984, **34**, 671-82.

Feldstein, Martin, 'Inflation, Income Taxes, and the Rate of Interest: A Theoretical Analysis,' *American Economic Review*, December 1976, **66**, 809-20.

Lahiri, Kajal and Zaporowski, Mark, 'Inflation, Expectations, and the Real Interest Rate,' Presented at the meetings of the American Statistical Association, August, 1984.

Rapping, Leonard A. 'The Domestic and International Aspects of Structural Inflation,' in James H. Gapinski and Charles E. Rockwood (eds), *Essays in Post*

Keynesian Inflation (Cambridge, Mass : Ballinger, 1979).
—— and Bennett, Stephen, 'Reflections on the Interest Rate,' Project on Economic Restructuring, University of Massachusetts-Amherst, July 1983.
Tanzi, Vito, 'Inflationary Expectations, Economic Activity, Taxes, and Interest Rates,' *American Economic Review*, March 1980, **70**, 12-21.
Wilcox, James A. 'Why Real Interest Rates Were so Low in the 1970's,' *American Economic Review*, March 1983, **73**, 44-53.

8 Economic Policy and the International Market: The Interest Rate and Third World Debt*

INTRODUCTION

The global economic decline of the early 1980s not only threatens the internal political cohesion of many nations, but it threatens the financial and commercial relationships among nations. Substantially lower interest rates would assist in stemming the tide of economic decline within the United States, and a cessation of economic decline in the United States would help immensely in providing some stability in a very precarious world situation. Moreover, the world trading system is threatened by the overhang of international debt that has accumulated over the past decade, and lower interest rates would significantly ease the very difficult problem of negotiating a debt settlement among private banks, depositors, taxpayers, international financial agencies and Third World borrowers.

The interest rate on dollar-denominated assets is only one of many financial matters relevant to American financial policy and the international marketplace. A stable internationalized trading system requires a financial system with appropriate international regulatory agencies that can achieve cooperation among nations on such matters as interest rates, exchange rates and international credits. The current efforts to avoid default on international bank loans and to accommodate countries with balance-of-payments deficits by expanding the International Monetary Fund's (IMF's) lending capacity to $90 billion with contributions from many

From Joseph V. Julian (ed.), *US Competitiveness in the World Economy* (Syracuse, NY, Syracuse University, 1984).

countries, including a US contribution of over $8 billion, is a wise but temporary solution to the problem of financing international trade. However, until longer-term financial agreements can be negotiated, short-term and partial solutions of this kind are required.

SOME INITIAL CONSIDERATIONS

Under reasonably stable political and military circumstances both at home and abroad, the Federal Reserve Bank significantly affects the ability and willingness of banks to make loans, and by so doing it influences the process whereby financial markets determine interest rates. Under these circumstances, the interest rate is a policy instrument that can be used to achieve both national and international economic objectives. However, under unstable circumstances, the Fed's authority is substantially circumscribed. In this instance, the national and international financial markets determine interest rates, with the Fed having precious little say in the matter. Of course, when such a situation prevails, authorities other than the Fed may become important, for there still remain other policy instruments. National and international policy objectives can be pursued by budgetary policy, regulatory policy, incomes policy, propaganda policy, military policy, industrial policy or, indeed, by a 'do nothing' or 'wait and pray' policy.

There is considerable disagreement over the appropriate mix of policies and strategies in the current economic situation. With the United States both economically and politically repositioning itself in a rapidly changing world economy, and with the outcome of this process necessarily uncertain because of the significant military, political and economic risks involved – e.g. large-scale war is an ever-present threat, and financial collapse and a further decline in domestic and world-trade are real possibilities – many Americans think it appropriate to manoeuvre through the crisis with cooperation, coordination and regulation. This view embodies the belief that with considerable effort our political process can achieve direction, reliability and coherency even in an unsettled world. Proponents of this view are committed to negotiating processes and a search for consensus.

On the other hand, the supporters of deregulation and unfettered markets prefer to manoeuvre through the crisis with each separate corporate, union and government bureaucracy making independent decisions in a market area. In this view, consensus is a chimera; the reserve army of labour is necessary to discipline recalcitrant midwestern workers; the reserve army of oil is required to punish OPEC for its excesses; and the reserve army of unpaid debts is necessary to embarrass overexuberant international bankers. Regardless of whether one endorses the unfettered market view or the regulated market view, the interest rate is a variable that can facilitate adjustment if, indeed, it can be significantly influenced by public authorities.

SOME FACTS ON RECENT INTEREST RATE BEHAVIOUR

With one important exception, short-term interest rates on three-month treasury bills were in the 12 to 16 per cent range between the beginning of 1980 and June of 1982.[1] This exception was the short period of credit controls between the spring and summer of 1980, a time when the short rate fell sharply from 15 to 7 per cent. However, after relaxing controls they returned to their previous high level.

In the three years preceding the extraordinary increase in interest rates that occurred in the winter of 1979–80, there was a trend increase in these rates. Between early 1977 and the historic announcement by the Fed in October of 1979 that it would take a restrictive stance by shifting from interest rate to 'money supply' targets, the short-term interest rate rose from slightly under 5 per cent to about 9 per cent.

Despite this trend towards increasing interest rates, many, indeed most, have attributed the rapid rise in interest rates in late 1979 and early 1980 to Fed orchestration. That this increase followed the shift in October of Fed policy gives some credence to this contention. However, this attribution ignores both the effect of the evolving international crisis and the progressive undermining of the Fed's authority after the breakdown of the Bretton Woods system in the early 1970s.

THE INTERNATIONAL FINANCIAL CRISES OF 1978 AND 1980

In the autumn of 1978 and again in the winter of 1980, there was panic in international financial markets. Both episodes were associated with the political and military situation in the Middle East. In both periods the dollar and dollar-denominated assets were sold in flight from American dollar. In both periods the dollar began a meteoric descent against the Japanese yen and the West German mark while gold prices and interest rates rose. In a two-week period during October of 1978, the dollar fell 14 per cent against the mark and 7 per cent against the yen. Gold rose from $225 an ounce to over $248 an ounce. Interest rates rose rapidly. This flight from dollar-denominated assets was even more intense during the winter of 1980.

Between December 1979 and February 1980, there was pressure on paper of all origins. Gold rose against all currencies. The dollar price of gold reached $850. Again, the dollar fell precipitously against the mark and yen, and the three-month treasury bill rate went from 12 to 15 per cent in only a two-month period. These events were responses to the Iranian revolution, the seizure of the American hostages in Iran, the increase in oil prices, the Soviet invasion of Afghanistan and the threat of nuclear war. Fear and anxiety precipitated an irrational flight from the dollar.

High short-term interest rates arrested the decline in the exchange value of the dollar as international banks, industrial corporations, foreign central banks and others were induced to hold dollar-denominated, short-term assets. Not only was the decline in the exchange value of the dollar stopped, it was reversed. Moreover, the flight to gold ended and gold prices tumbled.[2] A full-scale international monetary débâcle of 1930s proportions was averted.

These international considerations dominated the thinking of central bankers as they manoeuvred through the second oil crisis revolving around the fall of the Shah of Iran. The unstable and unpredictable psychology of the financial markets created an environment in which the Fed could not easily moderate the movement of interest rates. Any effort to lower rates would have required the Fed to 'eat' an incredibly large quantity of bills, which might well have precipitated a decline in the dollar, a run-up in gold prices and intensified speculation in real estate. Under these unstable conditions, it was not the Fed but rather international money markets that determined interest rates.

Since the summer of 1982, the three-month bill rate has fallen from about 12 to 8 per cent; from its peak in mid-1981 of about 16 per cent, the bill rate has been about halved. However, it is important to remember that the inflation rate has been more than halved over the same period; and, while we cannot easily measure the expected real rate of interest, we do know that the nominal interest rate has fallen by less than the inflation rate. Despite the significant decline in nominal interest rates, inflation-corrected interest rates remain at historically unprecedented levels.[3]

FINANCIAL INNOVATION

During the past decade the international financial system has
changed from a highly regulated system dominated by quasi-public
domestic and multinational financial and commercial agencies to a
less regulated system dominated by private banks. In the earlier
system the multinational agencies like the IMF, in conjunction with
central banks and treasuries, regulated exchange rates and the flow
of international credits. This orderly and regulated arrangement has
evolved into a system of floating or gyrating exchange rates,
unregulated Eurodollar markets and private bank loans to countries
with trade deficits. These international banking developments have
been matched by equally momentous changes in domestic financial
markets. Liability management, lines of credit, commercial paper,
trade credit, money market funds, NOW accounts, sweep accounts
and defections from the Federal Reserve system reflect these
domestic changes.

This new, evolving arrangement is one in which power and
authority are dispersed. A new process now governs the
international financial system. The system involves the interplay of
more diverse, competitive forces than existed under the old Bretton
Woods system. This new, emerging system suffers from all the
instability problems of an unregulated banking system operating in
a militarily and politically disordered global system. It is in this
context that one must analyse the current problem of high interest
rates.

With large-scale financial innovations, the money multiplier
analysis in which the Fed controls the money supply and, hence, the
credit supply by the manipulation of bank reserves, is no longer
applicable. Nor can we appeal to the argument that the Fed controls
expectations concerning future general business conditions and
hence the willingness of banks to lend. Authority is too dispersed
for the Fed to have this power.

Under these circumstances, the Federal Reserve Bank controls
neither the interest rate nor the supply of credit. The national and
international financial markets do that. The banks, the industrial
corporations, the central banks and treasuries of the industrialized
and oil-rich nations, and some millions of small savers expressing
themselves in financial markets are the principal actors in the
upward spiral of interest rates since late 1979. It is this unfettered
global market, not the Federal Reserve Bank, that is responsible for
high interest rates.

THE INTEREST RATE AND THE FINANCIAL MARKETS

To argue that the market and not the Fed determines interest rates is to raise the questions posed by Keynes in the 1930s as to how it is that markets set these rates. When the return on investment in physical capital becomes uncertain in the face of political and military disorder, long-term calculation loses its appeal, and it is short-run profits and speculation that attract the players and their money. In this instance, the long-term interest rate is no longer anchored by calculations based on the net gains from successfully organizing the bureaucratic infrastructure necessary to produce and distribute commodities efficiently. Instead, the long-term interest rate becomes a psychological variable subject to the 'hidden forces' that buffet the moods of financial speculators.

In normal times there is a widespread belief that tomorrow will not be too different from today. The recent past provides the conventional basis upon which to judge the future. But in abnormal times, when people feel threatened, there is no basis for the individual to engage in orderly extrapolation. In these circumstances, the anxious quest for a safe asset in an uncertain world, one in which the very idea of safety is a contradiction, governs the buy-sell decisions. A herd instinct or mass psychology dominates market behaviour. In this instance, the interest rate is a result of a market process, but this process is only seemingly based on decentralized planning and decision-making. The process is actually subject to a group mind, and the decentralized units behave as one. It is mass psychology, not neat and orderly marginal calculations, that determines these rates. Under these unstable conditions, market prices are subject to wide swings because demanders or suppliers are themselves subject to rapid changes of mood and mind. For all intents and purposes, interest rates can be at any level. However, once they rise relative to the rate of inflation, the markets may become accustomed to high returns and it will be difficult to lower them.

The similarity of underlying causes of instability in a financial process and in a political process under conditions of confusion and fear is useful to recognize. In both the political system and the financial system, the destruction of the basis for rational calculation or conventional extrapolation leads to unstable and unpredictable behaviour. It is in just such an environment that the social actors in both financial and political systems seek magical explanations for phenomena that are no longer explicable in the terms of rational considerations based on the extrapolation of a more peaceful past. In these instances a mass psychology takes hold.

In a scientifically-oriented society, one would expect that those who can package a seemingly scientific prediction of events subject to mass psychology – say, the interest rate or the inflation rate or the outcome of an election – would find a wide and receptive audience. However, as uncertainty continues and even the strong of heart lose confidence in rational and widely understood prediction procedures, there is a turning from procedural and impersonal authority, either in the hope that individuals with unique insight, with the 'gift of grace', can see the future, or simply because of the unconscious desire to be taken care of. Of course, before turning to personal authority there will be experimentation with new and untried rational procedures.

RECENT DEVELOPMENTS

In recent years we have seen this process operate in financial markets. In time, the bureaucratic financial organizations, which are the main participants in these markets, adopted a 'money supply' model of interest rates.[4] Excessively large increases in M1, the sum of currency and demand deposits, were taken as an indication that inflation rates would rise, and as a consequence, interest rates would also rise. Thus, when M1 rose too rapidly, bond prices fell, and, consequently, interest rates rose. The validity of widely accepted models became self-fulfilling. Later, the financial market participants shifted to a new model of interest rate determination, the deficit model. Large federal deficits, which meant a disarticulated political process as well as large financial needs on the part of the government, were assumed to cause high interest rates. Therefore, it was argued that a decline in the deficit would lower interest rates.

More recently, a decline in interest rates has been associated with statements by certain individuals. This suggests a willingness to abandon rational predictive models in favour of personal authority. There are analogous developments in the political system. Pollsters have found it increasingly difficult in recent years to get a fix on election outcomes, a sign that voters have become more confused about underlying issues and swayed to a larger extent than usual by personalities and image rather than substance.

SUMMARY OF INTEREST RATE DETERMINATION

At a time when asset preferences are unstable, when fear and anxiety rather than optimism and calm dominate the portfolio choices, when rumour and supposition supplant careful intelligence work and firm calculation, the task of a central bank is extraordinarily difficult. An inappropriate phrase at an inopportune moment can cause a stampede, a race for safety in a world in which there is no safety. The unexpected and large-scale application of mechanical controls, such as open market purchases of short-term securities, can panic the financial markets rather than lower the interest rate in an orderly way. Under these circumstances, the rapid twists and turns of the financial markets will seriously weaken a central bank's ability to control, or indeed, even significantly to influence, short-term interest rates.

With good alternatives to short-term dollar-denominated assets, the possibility of a flight to these alternative assets can neutralize the efforts of the Fed to regulate interest rates. In recent years numerous assets have served this role, including short-term foreign currency-denominated assets, gold, silver, common stocks, land and real estate. The Fed is faced with the possibility of substantial 'bear' resistance if financial markets have good alternatives to short-term paper.[5]

One might prefer to think of this problem in a way different from the portfolio adjustment view just expressed. High long-term interest rates can be attributed to uncertainty concerning inflation or the possibility of bankruptcies and defaults. Arbitrage – borrowing short and lending long – might then pull up the short rate. This process is not without risk, as the principals at First Philadelphia can attest.

Another approach might prove enlightening. Consider the flow demand and supply of short-term paper. Assume that the market has a firm belief that short-term rates will remain high, a belief perhaps rooted only in the fact that short-term rates have been high for a while. Then, an effort by the Fed to lower these rates by increasing its demand for short-term paper might encounter a neutralizing effort by corporate and consumer borrowers to borrow now rather than later. This would prevent the Fed from successfully levering short-term interest rates.

The interest rate is sometimes an instrument of national economic policy. In this instance the Fed has the authority and power as well as the technical capability to monitor the credit markets and if necessary to discipline recalcitrant participants. In other periods the interest rate is governed by many uncoordinated decisions – that is, by what is called the market. We now live in an era in which the interest rate is determined in both national and international financial markets, and in which the Fed can neither control nor significantly influence the course of these rates unless it is willing to use sledgehammer techniques. The private banks, the multinational corporations, the central banks and treasuries of industrialized and oil-rich nations, and the many thousands of middle-class savers who express their quest for rentier status through banks, insurance companies and money market funds, all of whom hold and trade in government and corporate securities– these are the principal actors in the upward movement of interest rates. It is this unfettered global financial market, not the Fed, that determines the course of interest rates. Those who blame the Fed for high interest rates invest this institution with more power and authority than it possesses. This search for regulatory order in unstable market processes is an understandable response to a disordered situation.

INTEREST RATES AND INTERNATIONAL DEBTS

While the interest rate is a matter of considerable national concern– it affects the distribution of income, the demand for homes and other consumer items, the carrying costs on the floating federal debt, and the level of capital expenditures – it is also a matter of major international concern, for it affects the carrying costs on the accumulated Third World debts, most of which are at floating interest rates. These debts have become political and economic fetters in the world trading system.

Debt involves a certain contradiction. If it is too burdensome to the debtor, trust and goodwill fade and the trading system is threatened. On the other hand, if it is eliminated without the acquiescence of the creditor, the trading system will also be threatened. This contradiction is an ancient problem. According to the 'Law of the Seventh Year' in Deuteronomy, indebtedness was automatically cancelled in the sabbatical year. However, when confronted with this law, the rich often refused to lend money to traders. Business stagnated. A variety of devices were suggested to avoid violating the laws while maintaining trade. The law known as 'Prosbul' (before the court) involved the execution of a document transferring the debt to the court. As a result, the 'Law of the Seventh Year' was not applicable to the transferred loan. Efforts to transfer international bank loans to the IMF may be seen by some as a modern-day Prosbul. The arrangement works only if the resulting terms are acceptable to both the borrowers and the lenders. Lower interest rates increase the probability of acceptance. Interest payments on Third World debts are co-mingled with domestic interest payments and used primarily to meet interest obligations on American dollar and Eurodollar bank deposits. The failure of borrowers to meet these interest obligations would create a cashflow problem for the banks. At lower interest rates on both loan and deposit accounts, the problem of nonperformance is lessened, and, by the same token, the problem of negotiating a settlement of these debts is eased. Let us consider the origin of these debts.

THE BRETTON WOODS SYSTEM AND THE FIRST OIL PRICE SHOCK

The essential financial organizing principle of the prosperous post-World War II era was established in the covenants of the Bretton Woods system. An abundant supply of credit was obtainable from international agencies and from the US Treasury, which at that time could successfully collect taxes. These credits were made available to accommodate deficit countries and, by the same token, to permit the long-run continuation of corresponding export surpluses, which facilitated domestic and global economic expansion. Under the Marshall Plan, the US Treasury provided the substantial funds that were necessary to maintain the flow of American exports to Western Europe. The public treasury replaced the private treasuries of the 1920s as the main source of international lending. Then, following the successful reconstruction of the Western European economies, the United States provided economic and military assistance to nations on the periphery of the Soviet Union and China, a programme that was the financial component of the American containment policy. From 1950 to 1973, the year of the oil crisis, some $150 billion in government funds were either lent or given to foreign governments. These trade credits supported accommodating governments around the world and provided a comfortable market for American as well as Western European and Japanese exporters.

With the phenomenal increase in oil prices and the accompanying enrichment of the oil-exporting countries, a new source of funds developed to accommodate deficit nations, which, it should be added, had their import costs increased by the hike in energy prices and their export sales decreased by the recession in the industrial countries that were the deficit countries' main markets. With the Americans now transferring billions to OPEC, US Treasury tax receipts were no longer an adequate or reliable source of foreign credits. In place of US government credits, the large private banks, in partnership with the oil exporters that had surplus funds – surpluses that were large, despite the increase by many OPEC nations in their importation of armaments, consumer goods and capital goods, and in their purchase of securities and real estate in the West – transferred these surpluses to deficit countries. The transfers were massive. When added to other trade surpluses that were deposited in the Eurodollar market, 70 per cent of the financing of trade deficits was now a private bank matter. These developments greatly increased the 'offshore' activities of the banks. In 1965, for example, US banks had about $20 billion in assets in their overseas branches. By 1978, this figure reached about $420 billion.

THE COMPLEX WEB OF DEBT

Thus, it was after the oil price increase of 1973 that the international banks developed to an art the practice of stimulating exports by the granting of hard currency loans from bankers to allegedly credit worthy Third World countries whose appetites for imports exceeded their abilities to pay.[6] The bankers utilized the technique of acquiring lendable funds by attracting deposits in the unregulated Eurodollar market, and they co-mingled these deposits with other sources of funds. The banks served either as intermediaries between borrowers and lenders – charging, of course, the usual middleman's fee – or as creators of new money. This latter act of monetary procreation has for centuries been the monopoly of those financial institutions most comfortably situated *vis-à-vis* the crown, the treasury, or the printing press.

There were borrowers throughout the world. The Eastern Europeans borrowed from German and other banks; the Latin American countries of Argentina, Brazil and Mexico sought credit accommodation from the American and other banks; the countries of East Asia borrowed from American and Japanese banks; the African nations borrowed from Western European and American banks. Representing themselves as well as the countries with export surpluses, the international banking institutions were anxious to accommodate. So long as there was modest global expansion the borrowers could and would pay simple and even compound interest, although no thoughtful banker was foolish enough to demand the repayment of principal, since such a demand would probably have terminated this mutually profitable arrangement.

This process of credit expansion created a market for exports to Eastern Europe, Latin America and elsewhere for West German, French, American and Japanese manufactured goods, as well as for OPEC's oil. The West was willing to exchange commodities for promises. Their ability to produce and their willingness to export in exchange for promises was an important reason for the modest growth following the sharp 1974–75 economic decline.

Are the Debts Excessive?

The debts accumulated by Eastern Europe and the non-oil-producing Third World nations are large but not necessarily excessive. In many instances, they are no larger than the debts incurred by the more voracious borrowers of prior eras that utilized British and other credit – India, China, Japan, Australia and Canada.

In some statistical sense these earlier debts may have seemed large, just as many of the current debts appear overextended when viewed statistically.[7] But there is no mechanical statistic that can capture the subtlety of the relationship between an international borrower and an international lender. Paradoxically, the debtor–creditor relationship is not so much an impersonal market relationship, based on monetary calculations and the power of compound interest, as it is a political relationship based on the commercial and military ties between debtors and creditors who are locked together in a system of exchange in which credit is the lifeblood of the arrangement. Principal may be rolled over, renegotiated or extended – at least until a war, a revolution or a depression eliminates it. Principal need never be repaid. Indeed, even interest payments can often be deferred; if not, they can be covered by some third party, usually an important central bank or a rich treasury. When political discipline is maintained, the lenders can often count on the discretion of their large depositors or other partners not to embarrass them by untimely withdrawals, and on the central bank or the treasury to act a 'lender of last resort'.

Debt becomes excessive only when the lender loses confidence or faith in the borrower, and, as every member of an intimate partnership knows, a lender's confidence is a state of mind – an attitude towards the present and the future – that cannot concretely be captured by statistics purporting to measure the borrower's ability to repay. The ratio of annual interest obligations to the debtor's annual exports, a figure that has admittedly risen some fourfold for non-oil-producing Third World countries in the past decade (or the real interest rate relative to the debtor's economic growth rate – a relationship that in the current depression is uncomfortably divergent with real interest rates, significantly exceeding pathetically small if not negative growth rates), is not irrelevant. However, for any given value of these statistics, the lender's willingness to believe is shaped by custom and habit as well as by political and military events. These considerations are not easily captured in numerical visions.

ELIMINATING INTERNATIONAL DEBTS

Debts are often abrogated, defaulted on or otherwise avoided in the chaos, confusion and political disintegration of war, revolution or depression. During World War I this harsh method of settling accounts was used. Several Eastern and Southern European debtors defaulted on their obligations. This should not, however, be seen as a matter of any significant historical moment, for economic growth had ended and the lenders and borrowers had served their historic function of providing markets for the industrial surplus of the German and other European factories. Indeed, in many respects such merciful acts of book-balancing are occasionally necessary to eliminate the braking effect on growth of debt accumulated during an earlier episode of prosperity.

The need for periodically eliminating debt from the books – in our time, from the tapes – is usually a necessity when the growth process stops or slows. Elimination usually occurs by default, not renegotiation. This was the process during World War I and again in the 1930s when the Germans, the Latin Americans and others renounced their obligations. It is unfortunate that a more orderly procedure for debt elimination is not more commonly employed in the private markets. It would be preferable to use renegotiation and compromise rather than default and bankruptcy to cleanse the borrowers' books of red ink and the lenders' books of illusions. In any event, regardless of how a debt overhang is eliminated, the cleansing effect of its elimination should be recognized. For example, the international system experienced an unprecedented expansion of world trade facilitated by international credits after World War II. This arrangement would have been impossible if politically and economically destabilizing obligations were not eliminated during the Great Depression and World War II.

The situation after World War II is profitably compared to the unfortunate developments after World War I. This war brought forth an understandable but none the less vengeful demand by the French and their allies for reparations from the vanquished, and the misguided insistence by the American wartime suppliers of food and material that the Allies repay their war debts in full. These demands were embodied in the Versailles Treaty. Consequently, the world economy was rendered politically unstable by the uncollectable debt burden of the Germans to the French, of the French and Italians to the British, and of the British and French to the Americans.

The disastrous political and economic consequences of adopting the bookkeepers' mentality with regard to international obligations and expectations were exposed by John Maynard Keynes in his prescient 1919 book, *The Economic Consequences of the Peace*. With respect to debts, Keynes counselled compromise and reconciliation. Otherwise, the pre-World War I international trading system would be unreconstructable in the postwar years.

Similarly, there are profound reasons why we must adopt today, with respect to Third World debt, the accommodating strategy recommended by Keynes some 60 years ago. Our own economic difficulties will not be solved by a further deterioration in conditions throughout the Third World. Nor will the demise of these economies lessen the likelihood of a nuclear exchange, the event that all economic and political action must be designed to avoid. Indeed, quite the contrary is true: as the world economy slips into a decline of unknown depth, the threat of nuclear war is increased, if only because the all too numerous individuals who make up the command and control hierarchies of the nuclear forces will be subject to the emotional strains and propaganda excesses attendant upon economic failure. It would seem that American foreign and economic policy must have as its primary objective the reconstitution of some world economic order.

AN INTERNATIONAL TRADING SYSTEM

An international trading system requires a mechanism for surplus units to finance deficit units through public or private loans. If this transfer mechanism fails, then trade will decline or collapse. As a general proposition, there exist only modest possibilities for adjustment through international price level changes, exchange rate changes or income changes. In this century, historical experience suggests that without credits, the trading system is threatened. Unfortunately, when loans are based on the mentality of the accountant, there comes a time when the accumulated stock of debts and credits becomes a fetter. Once the lender loses confidence in the borrower, the voluntary lending process stops. This is the situation that now exists in the international economy. The process of credit-creation must be restored.

Current Third World Debts
By 1982 the accumulated stock of debts of the international borrowers exceeded $600 billion, more than half of which was owed to private banks. In turn, most of the private loans were floating-rate debt, and about half had a maturity of less than a year. The interest obligations on the private debt were about $40–45 billion a year. Since the early 1980s, when the export prices of the debtors fell relative to their import prices and when nominal interest rates rose, it has proven impossible for these borrowers to meet the interest payments on the debt. Public funds transferred through the IMF and the treasuries have been required. In effect, the private debt is being socialized on piecemeal basis.

The current effort is makeshift. A more permanent resolution would entail the transfer of these debts from the private banks to an international institution like the IMF. In this process the debt could be restructured, converting short-term loans into long-term loans. If, for example, the banks were given long-term bonds for their short-term debt, the interest costs to the Third World could be substantially reduced. Such an arrangement would require agreement among governments obligated to the IMF, Third World debtors, and banks that are acting on behalf of their depositors and stockholders.

Just as the interwar debts were not of themselves the cause of the Great Depression and the subsequent war – there were many other problems associated with the breakdown of the international system of labour specialization that occurred during and after World War I – so the current level of debts to the private banks is not of itself the cause of the current economic crisis. Nevertheless, it is a source of political disagreement and economic friction. When interacting with other problems associated with the unstable global system, it can exacerbate conflict or prevent accommodation. Therefore it is important, if the global system is to be stabilized, that these debts be renegotiated without at the same time constipating the flow of credit to countries with trade deficits. As in the 1930s, the alternative to renegotiation is default and the possible breakdown of the international financial system. Lower interest rates would facilitate renegotiation.

CONCLUSIONS

Several conclusions follow from this discussion. I should stress, however, that in the current unsettled global environment, it is only possible to make limited and partial policy adjustments in response to particular problems. Broader policy adjustment, which would involve the accommodation of market and regulatory processes, must await the emergence of a political consensus both at home and abroad.

First, public authority must replace private authority in decisions regarding the transfer of funds from surplus to deficit units. The transfer of existing surpluses and the creation of additional funds is a matter best vested in an international clearing house or a global central bank. This institution must coordinate central bank policies as they affect domestic interest rates. It must achieve reasonably stable exchange rates. Without stable exchange rates, or an orderly process for adjusting exchange rates, foreign exchange speculation substantially weakens the ability of the Fed and other central banks to regulate domestic credit conditions.

In addition, efforts must be made to discourage speculation in gold, common stock, real estate and other assets and to increase the relative attractiveness of fixed-income securities. While this is ultimately a matter of stability in the global military and political situation, the central banks must selectively penalize excessive speculation while at the same time continuing their lender-of-the-last-resort function. This process would be facilitated by legal limits on interest rates and restrictions on certain types of credit. These are useful tools in the hands of the monetary authorities, especially if discretionary application is possible. Of course, these changes presuppose an appropriate political base for central bank action.

Finally, national and multinational institutions must avoid international default on private and public debt by continuing to fund deficit countries, but they must do so only on the condition that a serious renegotiation of the accumulated international debts is undertaken. This negotiation process involves taxpayers, depositors, private banks, central banks, treasuries, international agencies and borrowers. To facilitate the process of searching for agreement, much lower real interest rates would be immensely helpful.

NOTES

1. Throughout this paper I shall index interest rates by the short-term rate as measured by the three-month treasury bill rate. As a general proposition, most other important rates have moved roughly in sympathy with this rate. I have in mind, for example, the Corporate Aaa bond rate, the long-term treasury security rate, the FHA mortgage rate, the commercial paper rate and the Eurodollar rates. Because of uncertainty over inflation and default, the long-term markets have not been especially active. High interest rates in these markets are often attributed to this uncertainty. However, it is the movement of the short-term rates which has been the subject of intense speculation, imaginative theorizing and free-wheeling conjecture.
2. On a trade-weighted basis, the dollar was back to its 1973 levels by June of 1982 while the price of gold was at $350 an ounce. In addition, high interest rates broke the back of real estate and collectible speculation.
3. Over most of the post-World War II years the difference between the nominal interest rate and the current inflation rate was under 2 per cent. Today, the figure exceeds 5 per cent.
4. The fact that decision-making is a bureaucratic process, not the act of an individual, suggests an alternative interpretation for the popularity of economic models as the basis for decision-making. In the event of a mistaken financial judgement, the bureaucrat responsible for the decision can avoid this responsibility by shielding himself behind an economic model, provided, of course, the model has been established as a legitimate oracle.
5. The reader should not interpret these remarks as denying that short-term, real interest rates can fall. They can and might, especially if other assets like gold become unattractive. The argument here concerns the ability of the Fed to control real interest rates, not the inability of the market under appropriate circumstances to change real interest rates.
6. I trust that these comments will not be misinterpreted. I recognize that some of the loans to the Third World may have been diverted to the bank accounts or gold hoards of private parties. To this extent, the loans did not stimulate Western European or American exports.
7. The statistical view of repayment potential is misleading even on its own terms. Loans for consumption purposes unlike loans for physical investment do not provide for their own liquidation. It is difficult to judge, however, what fraction of the Third World loans were for productive purposes and, in any event, it would be difficult to determine whether future economic developments would vindicate the lender and absolve the borrower. Often it is unexpected or unusual developments which lead to the repayment of loans. For example, it was World War I and the British demand for agricultural and industrial goods, paid for by the selling of overseas assets, which wiped out a large part of Australian, Japanese, Canadian and American debts to the British. This was an unexpected windfall for the borrowers. Similarly, lenders sometimes hope that an unexpected development – oil discoveries in the North Sea or the Yucatan – will generate the means for repayment.

Part III:
Conclusions

9 In Search of the Economic Future*

INTRODUCTION

In these essays I have addressed many problems confronting the American and the world economy. The problems are too complex to be analysed in the framework of a simple model, regardless of whether it incorporates the political biases of the right or the left. Such models build cadre, not understanding. To clarify problems and outline solutions, it has proved necessary to draw eclectically from recent historical experience without reliance on one, simple framework. Those whose ideological positions impose consistency and order in a world where there is none, will recoil at my efforts. But human interaction is often intricate, sometimes emotional and frequently inconsistent. I apologize not for my effort, but for a recalcitrant world which does not divulge its secrets easily.

Social and economic problems are easier to identify than to solve. When behaviour is modifiable, a problem is solvable, at least in principle. But when the problem results from culturally or genetically ingrained thought processess through which undesirable behaviour is generated, private or collective efforts at palliation will be frustrated. In these instances, public policy is either useless or harmful. The world is a mixture of situations that can be changed and situations that cannot be changed. Most of the time, we muddle through, solving problems when possible and living with them when necessary. The trick is to classify problems properly into those that we can deal with and those that require political calm and luck. The

*Written in December 1987

goal is to avoid the social and economic tragedy of events like the Great Depression.

To the extent that important policy puzzles can be understood, manoeuvring through these difficult times will be facilitated. To pursue this goal, it is necessary to examine particular as well as general problems. The overriding problem is how best to develop an efficient and fair system of economic organization. In addressing this issue, I have tried to keep in mind that human history is the constant struggle between the forces of altruism and justice as opposed to the forces of self-interest and partiality. Although undoubtedly disappointing to many, a productive and hard-working society cannot be based solely on justice and brotherly love. Nor can a just and decent society be based solely on unregulated self-interest. One is a society of saints, the other of combatants. Neither is socially viable.

Under the umbrella of this broad issue, we are faced with a collection of specific problems. They include budget and trade deficits that are cyclically large and secularly growing, real wages that are stagnating, a productivity performance that is dis-appointing, a financial structure that is teetering, and an assignment of living standards that is destabilizing. While the first four of these problems have very little to do with the emergence of open as opposed to regulated markets, the deregulation movement of the 1970s and 1980s has exacerbated the problem of financial instability and it has skewed unfairly the distribution of economic welfare.

BUDGET AND TRADE DEFICITS

The United States is in the sixth year of an economic expansion, the longest in twentieth century history. This expansion has been driven by an enormous budget deficit coupled with the willingness of both corporations and consumers to borrow and spend. Combined with constrained growth abroad, this expansion has contributed to a growing trade deficit for it has provided the purchasing power necessary to finance imports without a corresponding growth in exports. Not only has the budget deficit encouraged imports, but it has tended to shift economic activity in favour of government and private consumption at the expense of investment. Appalled at the consumption party that has resulted, there has been an intense effort to convince voters, Congress and the Executive that the budget deficit must be reduced.

Since the budget deficit emerged under the impetus of large tax cuts and increased government spending in the early 1980s, it is properly perceived that reversing this fiscal pattern is necessary to reduce the deficit. Unfortunately, this requires a consensus on policy, something not so easily achieved in the current American political environment.

While a reduction in the budget deficit is probably desirable, caution is required in this matter. Remember, this deficit provided the world economy with Keynesian stimulus when it was needed. The United States was a market for distress goods and for a while both consumption and investment were stimulated. However, now that the domestic economy is near full employment, the budget deficit might well have become a drag on the economy in the sense that it encourages government and private consumption at the expense of investment. However, an ill-timed or too rapid an elimination of the budget deficit could create a domestic recession rather than stimulate investment, discourage imports and calm world financial markets.

Unfortunately, unless it reduces purchasing power by creating a recession, the manipulation of the budget deficit is an uncertain and unreliable vehicle for affecting the trade deficit. Even if a reduction of the budget deficit did not contain the growth in economic activity and even if it encouraged investment at the expense of consumption, there is still no obvious reason for the trade deficit to decline. After all, the proportion of GNP that is invested is about equal to the proportion of imports that are investment goods, which means that there is no simple mechanical way for a reduction in the budget deficit to correct the trade situation.

Admittedly, were the interest rate to fall in response to a fall in the budget deficit, this would mildly discourage financial capital inflows which, in turn, would cause a modest fall in the value of the dollar. This would provide some help on the trade deficit but hardly enough to matter. The recent, massive depreciation of the dollar indicates that we hardly require a reduction in the budget deficit to change the value of the dollar.

In any event, the interest rate will not automatically fall in sympathy with a decline in the budget deficit unless expectations of falling interest rates were created by the event. Under these circumstances, the Federal Reserve could take action to lower the interest rate as an offset to the depressing aggregate demand effect of a falling budget deficit. However, without such expectation, I doubt whether the Federal Reserve Bank has the power or authority to affect the interest rate significantly, a proposition that has been a central theme in many of these essays.

Recession is the link between a reduced budget deficit and a reduced trade deficit. But recession is costly in terms of output and jobs. Quite properly, then, some other, and less painful, medicine is needed, unless we are willing to let the trade deficits continue. However, persistent borrowing from abroad has drawbacks. While parties to a loan transaction often recognize that they must compromise because the failure of a debtor is simultaneously the failure of the creditor, debtors are inherently in the weaker position of the two. The history of debt as well as the wisdom of the ages supports this observation. In the current situation, America's international political and economic position is weakened by its international obligations. Moreover, even if we could cope with these repercussions on international power relations, foreign loans must eventually be repaid. This requires future exports which imposes a burden on future generations.

Two alternative policy medicines thought to be less painful than recession are often considered to curing the ills of the trade deficit, dollar depreciation and trade protection. These are believed to be fast acting cures at least relative to the remaining alternative, that of increasing productivity, improving the quality of our products and developing new, exportable products and processes. In this latter approach, workers and managers must be trained and motivated while technology must be stimulated. This takes time.

What are the prospects for a rapid improvement in the trade balance? Dollar depreciation can at best contain but not eliminate the trade deficit. Moreover, this price adjustment process works slowly. After almost three years of a falling dollar, the effects are still not very great. None the less, they have advantages over the only other short-run alternative, duties, quotas and other restrictions on trade.

Not unlike dollar depreciation, legislating and administering trade protection is a ponderous process with an uncertain outcome that at best will contain, not eliminate, the trade deficit. To the extent that they are even effective, both depreciation and protection increase the cost of imports and reduce immediate living standards. In the current political environment, exchange rate adjustments are probably on balance less partial and more flexible than trade protection. For this reason they are to be preferred. The current Trade Bill before Congress provides us with some insight into the politics of protection.

The current bill contains provisions on matters of importance but irrelevant to restraining imports. These include required advance layoff notice, education grants and the reporting of foreign investment holdings in the US. While these issues need not concern us here, their existence in the bill demonstrates the difficulty of surgically introducing protection.

The proposed trade bill would weaken the authority of the President in the protection granting process under US trade law and it would alter the rules under which the US Trade Commission makes its determinations. In matters of alleged unfair trade, or alleged dumping or alleged imports subsidization, the proposed law would increase the number of cases brought before the US Trade Commission. It would also increase the likelihood of duties or quotas being introduced in any particular case. However, until administrative and court law develops, it is difficult to anticipate the degree of protection that these provisions represent. The bill is protectionist, but probably less so than the opposition contends. It demonstrates that the US is in no position to develop a calibrated and refined squeeze on its foreign competitors.

The trade deficit, the depreciating dollar and the call for protection are evidence of a decline in the global competitiveness of American industry. While the discussion of depreciation versus protection is of some immediate interest it does not address the main problem. In the final analysis, our uncomfortable trade situation reflects the weakness of American technology and productivity, the root cause of our inability to achieve trade balance and, it should be added, of our failure to achieve adequate real wage growth. It is in the production sphere where America has faltered.

While living standards depend on the productivity of our people in producing both tradeable and nontradeable goods, international competitiveness depends not just on our productivity in the export sector, which is mostly manufactured and agricultural products as well as raw materials, but on our ability to create new and high quality exportable products and processes, and on our ability to improve the quality of existing products. These capabilities depend on individual motivation and attentiveness, and on the spread of hard technology. Culture and training determines individual behaviour. Research and development determines the advances and spread of hard technology. Often it is necessary for the military to be the sponsoring agency for support of the technology.

REAL WAGES, TECHNOLOGY AND PRODUCTIVITY

Real wages have been stagnant in the United States for fifteen years. Except for the recent improvement in manufacturing productivity, a sector where tradeable goods are produced but where only 20 per cent of the employees work, overall productivity has been stagnant for well over a decade.

Private investment is a vehicle for introducing new processes and methods. Adequate levels of investment require a stable and expanding level of economic activity and a high proportion of GNP devoted to investment. It is widely believed that the US consumes too much and invests too little. I share this judgement but fear that this will be a difficult situation to rectify.

Because the United States is a mature economy it is not surprising that the percentage of its gross and net national product which is currently invested is lower than it had been in the years of its initial industrial expansion, 1865–1914. It is also lower than the investment levels in Japan and West Germany, two countries devastated by the war, and currently major economic competitors. The American investment rate is also low when compared to that of the newly industrializing nations of East Asia which, like the United States in the nineteenth century, are in the early stages of industrialization.

Were the relatively low investment rates in the United States simply a reflection of its late stage of industrialization, there would be little that could be done about America's international competitiveness and its slowly growing wages. However, Germany and Japan are mature economies which recovered from their war losses many years ago, but which still devote much higher shares of their net national product to net investment than does the United States. Moreover, in the United States, net investment relative to net national product is lower in the 1980s than it was in the 1950s and 1960s. There would appear to be some room for improvement in this matter.

A move toward balancing the federal budget will not automatically correct the investment problem. A tax increase and a reduction in military and entitlement expenditures will restrain the desire to consume, especially if we introduce some form of a national sales tax and a special tax on the use of oil. But reducing the claims of government and consumers on economic resources does not automatically stimulate investment. A lower interest rate might help but neither through market forces nor through the action of the Fed is this likely to happen. In any event it won't be enough. While residential housing demand might be interest sensitive, investment in fixed plant and equipment is not.

While investment tax credits and accelerated depreciation allowances might help to stimulate investment, more direct action is required. Government spending must be redirected to rebuild the public infrastructure including roads, bridges, and water and sewer systems. More government financing of R & D is required. More engineers and scientists must be trained while businessmen must be made more familiar with and receptive to new ways of doing things even if they are risky. In particular, managers and others must be encouraged to invest in real, not paper assets. Devising tactics to arrest the takeover movement will help in this regard.

Some thought must also be given to investment in education and training. With some federal assistance, state and local governments spend about $500 billion a year in gross investment on formal education and training. To this must be added very large but unrecorded corporate spending on training workers at the job. However, even the recorded expenditures are larger than current gross investment spending for private nonresidential investment in physical capital, about $450 billion a year. Investment in education along with investment in physical capital is clearly an important alternative to consumption.

There is a desperate need to improve the problem-solving, numerical reasoning and written communication skills of new labour force entrants. However, the self-discipline, family encouragement and community support necessary to sustain the learning process has been undermined by a generation of neglect, broken families and community disintegration. We have paid a price for our social liberalism and our libertarian values. Under these circumstances, it is difficult for even motivated local school boards and teachers to generate the enthusiasm and commitment necessary to improve the learning process. Instead funding from the current large state budget surpluses might not be enough to surmount these difficulties.

The increased investment necessary to improve productivity, combined with the reduction in imports and increase in exports necessary to reduce the trade deficit, implies a large decline in the rate of growth of American consumption per capita, a growth rate that is already low by post-World War II standards. In absolute terms, a $150 billion reduction in the trade deficit and a $50 billion increase in investment means a $200 billion decline in consumption. This is a staggering $2400 decline in consumption per household per year. It implies a period of austerity and dangerous political currents, a subject that no political leader is capable of openly addressing. In democratic politics, the successful politician promises the moon even if only green cheese can be delivered. This is the lesson of President Carter's 1979 speech on the 'malaise' in

American society and of Senator Mondale's unsuccessful 1984 campaign for the Presidency.

THE EMERGENCE OF MARKET REGULATION

In the 1930s, the government's authority to regulate financial, labour and other markets was greatly expanded, the redistribution of income and wealth became a priority, and activist monetary and fiscal policy gained adherents. While these organizational changes did not end the Great Depression, the War did that, they were well suited to the coming prosperous post-war years when the United States broadly as well as specifically regulated its domestic economy and took a leading role in the regulation of international exchanges, trade and financial capital flows. Of course, post-war prosperity was created by fortuitous economic and political conditions, not by regulation, but regulation did assist in containing the worst aspects for unfettered markets, overbanking, speculation and the lopsided distribution of claims on economic resources.

The principle of domestic and international market regulation served the nation and the global economy quite well, at least until the early 1970s when the military failure in Indochina, the breakdown of the Bretton Woods arrangements and the first oil shock signalled the loss of American leadership in the world economy. Without a leader to forge and enforce international agreements, the international markets could not be managed. Governments were simply outmanoeuvred by financial innovation, swamped by massive private financial capital flows, overwhelmed by the difficulties of reaching trade agreements, and often unable to prevent the movement of people across borders. As a result, fixed exchange rates were replaced by gyrating exchange rates, government-sponsored international credit was replaced by private credit, government to government cooperation became more difficult and international corporations proceeded to move goods, jobs and direct investments without regard to national policies or goals.

Global economic growth slowed under the pressure of declining international cohesion. There was a need for a new international and domestic division of labour but this process could not be guided by collective decision-making. Not only were the international conditions unconducive to such an effort, but domestic conditions were also inauspicious. The Federal Reserve had much of its authority compromised, the Presidency was weakened, the

Congress was disorganized and the cohesiveness of the party system was undermined. Special interests gained sway and collective calculation was impossible.

MARKET DEREGULATION

By the late 1970s international financial markets were deregulated and the process of deregulating domestic banking, transportation, labour relations, racial relations, distributional arrangements and other aspects of domestic economic life was accelerating. Market authority was growing and political authority was declining. This development was blessed by President Reagan and praised by the proponents of free, unregulated markets. But these parties no more caused the rise of open markets than the morning sun. Under the circumstances, the market was the only social arrangement that could sustain economic activity. Many railed against it, but this posture was fruitless and increasingly irrelevant. Indeed, the deregulation process was a global event, one which included much of the developed and underdeveloped capitalist world and some of the communist world as well.

Unregulated markets promote self-interest and egotism. They depreciate altruism and civic spirit. While this unleashes the productive power of individual initiative, it does so at an alarming cost. Driven by the gambler's instinct and the 'get-rich-quick' ethos, the financial markets are destabilized, a situation that has always worried central bankers becuase it threatens the production and employment process. Meanwhile, living standards improve at an uneven rate, roughly commensurate with the uneven distribution in ability, cunning, financial inheritance and the drive for power, a situation that distresses men and women of good will. Not unlike the gambling problem, the distributional problem undermines the stability of the market process for it creates the widespread belief that the system is unjust and that redress requires the use of democratic political processes to restrain the market even if inefficiencies result.

Unstable Financial Markets
Both internationally and domestically, financial markets have been unstable since the early 1970s. They have been driven by speculative excesses. Asset prices are not anchored to slowly moving market fundamentals. Rather, they are driven by speculators speculating on the actions of other speculators. This is a formula for violent swings

in asset prices. Witness, for example, the large fluctuations in the value of the dollar in the 1980s, the behaviour of prices in many real estate markets during the same period and the meteoric rise in world stockmarket prices at the beginning of 1987 followed by their sudden collapse in the autumn of the same year.

Governments have had difficulty in dealing with these excesses. In international exchange markets, the central banks cannot always agree on concerted action. And, even when they do agree, they are often overwhelmed by expectational resistance and massive private capital flows. In an unregulated international financial market, the dollar is unstable for its movements are dominated by speculative financial capital flows, not by the movement of goods or the actions of the central banks.

If all that happened was that some speculators won while others lost, the whole affair would not be a matter of public concern. Unfortunately, this is not the case. Many are affected who are not involved in the speculative game. Among other things, profits and jobs are affected in regions of the country where domestic export and import-competing industries are buffeted by the resulting large and unpredictable swings in exchange rates.

Turning to domestic financial matters, the Federal Reserve Bank has great difficulty in controlling either credit or interest rates. Financial innovation including nonbank deposit creation and bank liability management have rendered velocity and the money multiplier unpredictable. Neither credit nor money can be controlled, at least at the present time. Witness the behaviour of velocity in this decade and the unstable behaviour of the M1 money supply when it was allegedly the target variable for Fed policy in the early 1980s.

Nor is the Federal Reserve Bank any more successful in regulating or setting interest rates than it is in controlling the money supply. It was the panicky flight from paper of all origins triggered by the second oil shock and the fall of the Shah, not the Fed, that drove interest rates so high in 1979 and 1980. And it has been the high expected real returns on speculative assets, not the Fed, that sustains the real interest rate in this decade. Even the sharp fall in interest rates which accompanied the stock market crash of 1987 was caused by a temporary private flight from stocks to bonds, not the Fed.

Of course, there are subtle matters of judgement involved in the issue of whether the Fed can significantly influence the interest rate for as I have argued in these essays, the interest rate is an expectational variable and its control requires control over expectations. Perhaps in the future the Fed will regain such control or perhaps there is more of it today than there was a few years ago. My only point is that the massive rise in nominal rates in the early years of this decade and the high level of real rates throughout the decade are market and not policy results.

One should not infer from these comments that the Fed is totally powerless. Indeed, in a sense it is all powerful for it possesses the financial equivalent of nuclear weapons. It is the lender-of-last-resort, the guarantor of liquidity for the entire financial system and the real muscle behind deposit insurance and the continued operation of insolvent banks. In fear of panicking the financial markets, the Fed has been hesitant to 'pull the plug' on many overextended financial institutions, an essential action but one that has encouraged the overbanking process.

To maintain confidence in the entire credit process, the Fed has acted in many different instances. It has used its great power in the 1984 Continental Bank crisis when it halted a run on the Chicago institution and perhaps the banking system in general. It used its power again in the days following the October 1987 stockmarket crash when it coordinated through implicit guarantees the large banks and other financial institutions, inciting them to provide credit to borrowers distressed by the suddenness of the fall in stock prices. It has assisted the Federal Savings and Loan Board which has guaranteed liquidity in the southwest where many savings and loans found themselves insolvent because of the unexpected fall in oil prices and their questionable lending practices.

The Distribution of Income and Wealth

There has been a lopsided shift in favour of the higher income groups in this decade. In the 1930s and 1940s, the nation achieved a much greater degree of equality than it had earlier. These gains eroded slowly after the end of World War II. This erosion process has probably accelerated in more recent years. Because wealth is so much more unequally distributed than income, the capital gains in both paper assets and housing are concentrated at the upper end of the income distribution and this has contributed to the consumption excesses of those who are relatively better off.

On the other hand, the growing inequality in the distribution of income, a statistic which does not include capital gains, has itself contributed to greater inequality in the distribution of consumption. However, much of this phenomenon in recent years has been the result of a rising proportion of two-earner families caused by an increasing number of working women and the rising proportion of single-worker families, headed mostly by mothers who are divorced or otherwise without partners.

THE REREGULATION OF FINANCIAL MARKETS

Some effort at reregulating international and domestic financial markets seems the proper policy direction to eliminate the worst abuses of current financial arrangements and to reduce the chances of a financial debacle. Unfortunately, at the present time the political foundation for such a development only faintly exists. It is difficult to imagine that the necessary international cooperation can be achieved. Nor is the Congress or the President predisposed to embark on such a course of action. The present alignment of political forces would make such proposals premature. In time, however, regulation might be politically feasible.

In this event, domestic legislation and Executive involvement should be designed to bolster the authority and nerve of the Federal Reserve and other regulatory institutions. The US objective should be to lead the effort to organize the international institutions necessary to assist in the reduction of trade imbalances and to stabilize exchanges. It must also be an objective to moderate speculation in domestic financial markets. Among other things, this will require increasing the Fed's influence over the supply of the means of payment, the supply of credit and the domestic interest rate.

In the international sphere, it would be desirable to achieve some coordination of national monetary and fiscal policies, a development which, among other things, might prevent the very unbalanced international budget deficit situation that developed in 1982 from recurring. Coordination would aid in balancing trade and stabilizing exchanges. Not only do balanced trade and financial flows require a synchronized rhythm among countries in internal inflation rates, interest rates and growth rates, but international cooperation makes moral suasion and market intervention more credible and effective tools for stabilizing exchanges. Unless the market participants believe that governments can and will persist in the effort to stabilize exchanges, they cannot be stabilized. Once stabilized, they can serve as a fixed point around which the international trading system can be organized.

International cooperation should be used for very broad institutional purposes. The stabilization of exchanges ultimately requires an understanding between markets and governments. Such an understanding could be based on a return to a Bretton Woods-type system or by a crawling peg designed to fix the real exchange rates. Unfortunately, it would not be easy to agree on or introduce such a system at the present time. In the interim, some less than optimal solution is necessary. In this regard, a tax on international financial transactions and an interest equalization tax would be helpful. These taxes coupled with some macroeconomic coordination and cooperative foreign exchange intervention might assist in discouraging foreign exchange speculation and reducing the current instability of exchanges.

However, even if international cooperation is unachievable, an effort should still be made to reregulate some activities in the domestic financial markets. While this effort might be compromised by the financial openness of the economy, the United States economy is very large and there are still a few degrees of freedom left. Indeed, we are probably more constrained by the high ratio of government debt to GNP, corporate debt to corporate equity and consumer debt to disposable income than we are by the interconnectedness of international financial markets. These high leverage ratios make the economy vulnerable to a recession and raise the risk of a cumulative financial decline. It is this situation that often forces the monetary authorities to accommodate when they would otherwise choose to restrain the system.

The reregulation of domestic financial markets will enable the Fed to establish greater influence over the interest rate, the supply of money and the supply of credit. However, neither the control of credit nor the interest rate is a mechanical matter. For example, influencing the interest rate requires much more than open market operations on the short end of the market and the manipulation of the federal funds rate. In the final analysis, interest rate control requires nothing less than the ability of the Fed to influence market expectations regarding the future course of interest rates, a process that is a matter of power and authority, not mechanical control.

Authority is a subject more suitable to the thinking of Machiavelli than Ricardo. Partly it is a matter of what we call charisma, something we sometimes seek in our leaders but do not always find. Partly it is a matter of institutional arrangements not always easy to develop.

Legislative mandates and Executive orders can bolster the power of the Fed. These actions coupled with the willingness and organizational capability of the Fed to act are crucial to its authority. Action itself increases authority, for authority exists when those over whom it is exercised believe that it exists. Nothing increases the credibility of a regulatory agency more than its ability and willingness to control the activities of the regulated. The precise nature of the intervention is often less important than the intervention itself.

By this proposition I do not mean to imply that any mindless or irrelevant regulation is respected or desirable. The regulatory action must be reasonable and purposeful. With regard to banking, it would seem appropriate that the regulatory agencies control the extent of bank mergers, the level of bank capital requirements, the ease of bank entry into different financial markets, the degree of interstate banking, the composition of bank earning assets, the accounting rules used by banks, margin requirements and consumer requirements on down payments.

To these ends, we must legislatively expand the domain of influence of the Federal Reserve, the Securities and Exchange Commission and other financial regulatory agencies. The objective should be to enable us to return to a financial system in which the means of payment is controllable and in which the overall credit creation process can be contained.

In this regard, the 100 per cent reserve proposals of the Chicago economists in the years just before and after World War II would seem a reasonable goal. Such an arrangement requires that the creation of unregulated checkable deposits be contained by either prohibition or by some other procedure for discouragement. In addition, explicit or implicit government deposit insurance should be sparingly applied to noncheckable bank and nonbank deposits. Banks should be required to mark assets to market and increased capital reserve ratios should be applied. The effective implementation of these and other changes designed to enhance the authority of the regulatory institutions will require concentrating the authority to regulate in the hands of fewer government agencies than now exist.

Efforts should be made to restrain directly gambling in the financial markets. In this attempt, it would be helpful to introduce high marginal tax rates on short term capital gains and a turnover tax in markets where bonds, commodities and stocks are traded. The volume of trading in financial markets would be reduced but this is the objective, not a matter for concern. After all, most corporate investment is financed by retained earnings, not through the stock or bond markets. The breadth and liquidity of these markets is not especially important to the investment process. However, such action might be a matter of concern to governments who issue bonds. Somewhat higher interest might ensue. But this effect should be small since the tax should apply to a wide range of financial assets.

There is a possibility that some financial activity would move abroad under the weight of a turnover tax. However, I do not think we should concern ourselves with the possibility that, say, London expands its casino business at New York's expense. However, we must be concerned with the possibility that a turnover tax would reduce the attractiveness of dollar denominated assets. This might discourage the holding of dollar denominated assets as an international reserve. Undoubtedly the reserve currency status of the dollar involves certain benefits. But it involves costs as well. Although in the final analysis the benefits might exceed the costs, it must be remembered that the world's banker must be the world's major industrial power and this consideration, not market liquidity, is the proper subject of our public discussion.

Excessive competition in financial markets often leads to excessively risky behaviour. Since there is already adequate competition in the markets serviced by banks, insurance companies, investment banks, mutual funds and stockbrokerage houses, added competitive pressures might simply stimulate added risk taking without any corresponding benefits in cost reduction. Efforts to reduce the geographic constraints on firms providing financial services and to increase competition among various types of financial institutions are best defeated. It remains useful to maintain restrictions on interstate banking and the balkanization of financial markets under the rules of Glass-Steagall.

A variety of financial activities like the trading in stock options should be restored to their rightful place, the Las Vegas casinos. They should simply be prohibited. The efficiency gains of many of these arrangements is more than offset by the disruptive effects of the gamblers who are attracted to many of our more useful financial markets.

In the end, increased financial regulation might not be politically feasible or, if feasible, unable to contain the speculative spirit. In this event, more draconian measures will be on the agenda. Recession usually contains overexuberant speculators and the overaccumulation of debt. But it is a risky development. Once in motion, an economic decline can snowball. The difficult choice we face in the trade-off between speculation and recession is similar to the choice that confronts us when we are faced with the trade-off between inflation and recession. In one instance the increased regulation of financial markets might help to avoid or moderate the recession while, in the other, wage and price controls might serve the same function.

THE DRIVE FOR FAIRNESS

Financial wealth is unevenly distributed. The upper 10 per cent of the families own 60 per cent of the cash, stocks, insurance and bonds. Housing is more evenly distributed, but still the very young and poor do not own houses. Inheritance taxes are the usual device for creating at least some degree of equality in opportunity. As an instrument of redistribution, the effectiveness of these taxes has been eroded in the United States. Inheritance taxes should be effectively increased and collected. Furthermore, the current $125,000 tax exemption on capital gains from the sale of private homes should be discontinued and we should discourage the quiet transfer of property to children from old or sick parents who then become a ward of the state.

Recent reductions in the marginal income tax rates and increases in the per cent of taxes collected from the social security payroll tax have compromised the progressivity of the federal income tax. A low-income wage earner now pays a 14 per cent federal income tax rate plus 7 per cent social security tax. A wealthy property owner now pays only a 28 per cent tax on income from rents, dividends, interest or capital gains. The principle of progressivity must be reestablished if we are to offset the uneven outcomes of the market.

The nation needs a value-added tax to assist in the war on consumption. Exempting clothing and food will assist in maintaining the principle of progressivity. It is especially important that the United States introduce an energy tax, for our conservation efforts have been greatly lessened since the fall in the relative price of energy. Another energy crunch would find the United States more vulnerable than necessary.

Of course, motivation is very important but there is little evidence that higher marginal tax rates will significantly lessen effort. People will work hard even if the stakes are small. Our current problem of motivation and attention is more a matter of culture than relative prices. As for the savings necessary to finance investment, most of it is done by the corporations in the form of undistributed corporate profits, not directly by households. We must encourage corporate savings and investment by continuing to reduce the tax on corporations and by inciting them to invest in physical capital, not paper assets.

Not only is a fairer tax system needed, but greater equity is required in the matter of government expenditures. Social Security benefits should be means tested. Training allowances and cash assistance should be provided to veterans of our production system who have been displaced by the global restructuring of industry. And, of course, cash assistance should be provided to those who have been emotionally and physically compromised by the strain of economic and social life.

Most importantly, we must provide for our children by reducing our trade deficit, encouraging investment and discouraging excessive consumption. This is the priority of our generation.

Index